The Legal Health Record

Regulations, Policies, and Guidelines

William Kelly McLendon, RHIA

Michael R. Lowe, Esq.
TECHNICAL EDITOR

AHIMA
PRESS

ISBN: 978-1-58426-258-9

AHIMA Product No.: AB121010

AHIMA Staff

Claire Blondeau, MBA, SENIOR EDITOR

Michelle Dougherty, MA, RHIA, CHP, DIRECTOR, PRACTICE LEADERSHIP

Katie Greenock, EDITORIAL AND PRODUCTION COORDINATOR

Ashley Sullivan, ASSISTANT EDITOR

Ken Zielske, DIRECTOR OF PUBLICATIONS

American Health Information Management Association
233 North Michigan Avenue, 21st Floor
Chicago, Illinois 60601-5809

ahima.org

Contents

CD-ROM Tools

Appendix of Forms and Definitions

Appendix of Table Tools

About the Author

William Kelly McLendon, RHIA, is the president and founder of Health Information Xperts, a consulting firm for electronic health records, electronic document management, and health information automation; and president and founder of Information Evolution Management, which provides EHR consulting and educational services to healthcare entities and vendors. At Eclipsys Corporation, McLendon served as VP, Clinical HIM Strategies; Director, Record Manager Domain; and Sales Executive. Prior positions include VP, Health Information Management; and Program Manager, Data Management Division, at MedPlus. His involvement with AHIMA spans 30 years, during which he has authored several articles, presented at national conventions, and served on several committees and task forces. In addition, he was the recipient of the AHIMA Visionary Award in 2003.

About the Technical Editor

Michael R. Lowe, Esq., has been board certified in health law by the Florida Bar, and is the managing partner of the healthcare law firm Michael R. Lowe, P.A., which serves clients throughout the state of Florida and nationally through affiliations in Georgia, Texas, Ohio, Illinois, and California. His primary areas of practice are healthcare law/litigation and medical malpractice defense. Lowe has been a board-certified health law attorney since 2004.

Preface

I undertook this project to create a reference work with a relatively narrow focus, that of explaining from a record manager's perspective, how to create and execute projects that result in medical records that are better organized and increasingly offer better legal defensibility. As the migration toward electronic records from older paper environments marches on, professionals responsible for addressing this evolution will find content that assists in meeting the challenges these changes bring to every healthcare provider and the court system. As you use the tools and strategies provided here, be mindful that you are straddling both the legal and record management and information technology arenas and may need to enlist help from other knowledgeable professionals. Lead and motivate those around you to get involved and work through the numerous processes necessary to clearly understand and organize your organizational strategies and workflows. Rest assured you can be successful with legal health record projects, and understand that your peers are successfully undertaking these same projects and facing the same challenges.

Kelly McLendon, RHIA
President, Health Information Xperts

Acknowledgments

The author wishes to thank Jim Braden, Mike Marable, and Kim Baldwin-Stried Reich for their invaluable contributions. Also to Chris Edwards, Chris Jordan, and many others granting me insight and experience that was so necessary in order to create this type of reference work.

Additional thanks to Michael Lowe, Esquire, for education on the deeper legal concepts and the thoughtful reviews of the material.

Of special note, Claire Blondeau and her team as well as Michelle Dougherty and all of the reviewers who worked hard to help produce a great product, thank you as well.

Chapter 1

Introducing Legal Health Records

Learning Points

- Describe primary and secondary uses of legal health records
- Know the difference between a legal health record and personal health record
- Understand that there is not a common definition of the term legal health record

Electronic health records (EHRs) are transforming the management of all types of healthcare records. New standards and practices are gradually evolving today's **medical records** from purely paper into increasingly electronic formats. Many healthcare providers have created what are referred to as **hybrid records,** which can be a mixture of paper and electronic or multiple types of electronic records. Other providers may or may not create hybrids, but are also on track to develop records that are almost completely electronic from creation to final destruction. This has proven to be an elusive long-term goal that probably will involve some amount of paper for years to come. Providers of care having electronic records that exclude paper, without at least scanning some documents, is unlikely in the foreseeable future. Certainly, the management of completely electronic healthcare records, with commonly adopted standards and practices, is the ideal goal of the electronic health record movement, which is being fostered by driving principals of patient safety and governmental programs and requirements.

An objective of this book is to provide readers with a thorough understanding of the concepts surrounding the term **legal health records** (LHR). This term has been created to describe the data, documents, reports, and information that comprise the formal

business record(s) of any healthcare organization that are to be utilized during legal proceedings. Understanding legal health records requires knowledge of not only what comprises business records that are used as legal health records but also the processes and the physical and electronic systems that manage these records. This work examines all of these areas to facilitate a complete understanding of the theory behind the LHR, and also includes hands-on tools to be used in bringing this theory into real practice. Additionally, key terms related to the LHR are **bolded** throughout the book.

While the general principles discussed here can be applied to many or most types of healthcare records, including medical records as opposed to financial or other internal business records, the actual documentation principals of a patient's care are not the focus of this work. Within this book we will also be highlighting the **health information management (HIM)**—otherwise known as the record management—perspectives on records to be used in legal proceedings. Many subjects can be classified as topical to the discussion of legal health records. For example, clinical documentation guidelines are important to the LHR, but this subject is not covered here in depth. The objective of this work is a more narrow scope surrounding record management attributes and processes, including how they are impacted by legal process usage. Clinical documentation *attributes* important to record management evaluation criteria of EHR systems are detailed, but the usage of these tools as *guidelines* is left to other references.

It is important to understand that this text is written by and for record managers and **custodians**. Legal concepts and principles are applied and relied upon for sound foundations for all of the concepts presented. While there are already several references available, full of legalese, in the marketplace for sophisticated readers that include attorneys, judges, and other administrative workforce members, this book concentrates on record management and custodial duties along with common tools that facilitate the performance of those jobs.

Business records for healthcare practitioners can take many forms. The hierarchy of records is summarized in figure 1.1.

While it has been recognized for years that patient safety is positively impacted by the technology advantages of EHRs, there has been fragmented and sporadic migration toward these electronic systems throughout the past two decades. The **Health Information Technology for Economic and Clinical Health Act or HITECH Act** (part of the ARRA; **American Recovery and Reinvestment Act of 2009**, also known as the Stimulus Plan) has fostered, with its incentive payment funding for adoption of **Meaningful Use of Certified EHRs**, a tightly focused set of targets for vendors and providers with a timeframe that requires concerted action that will significantly migrate many, if not most, providers of healthcare away from a paper-based to a much

Figure 1.1. Legal health record hierarchy

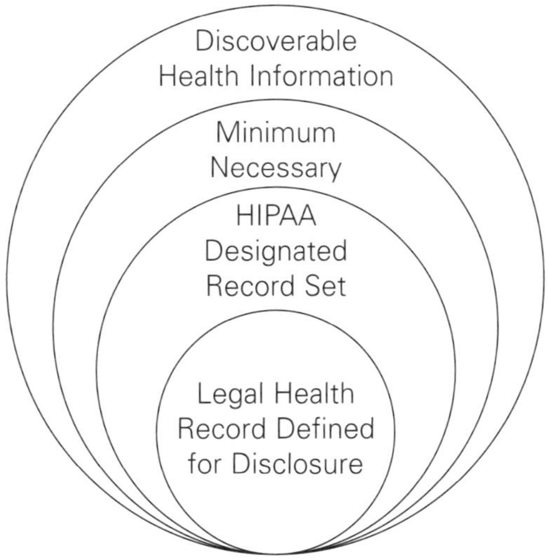

more electronic health record. According to Beaudoin (2009): "The first incentives will be paid in 2011 based on attestation by the provider of care that the Meaningful Use of Certified EHRs have been met. By 2015, physicians who are not using certified EHRs could be penalized by Medicare and Medicaid."

This migration from paper and hybrid medical records to more electronic records offers unparalleled opportunities for patient safety and care improvement, but also raises risks and challenges to everyone involved with the access, use, and overall management of these records.

Another dimension of change that opens realms of opportunity for cost reduction, quality, and effectiveness of care and patient safety is the goal of **health information exchanges (HIEs)** beyond the original, single medical record and provider of care. Ideally, these data exchanges and their facilitating infrastructures, such as **regional health information organizations (RHIOs)** and the **national health information network (NHIN)**, are all working to achieve the grand EHR goal of fully interconnected healthcare, where previous test results, medications, and treatments are available for each new provider's usage. This new dimension of healthcare brings its own record requirements and challenges, such as who will manage the as of yet ill-defined technologies required for fully interconnected data exchanges.

As if these previous changes were not enough, there is one more expansion evolving within the industry—**personal health records (PHRs)**. These records are very different in that patients store and retain their healthcare data (either in paper or electronic form), not the care providers. This is a significant change that must be addressed in the LHR equation as these PHRs are more fully developed, used by patients, and then incorporated into the more traditional provider EHRs. Many times, this incorporation of PHR data into an EHR may be solely for historical reference, which in reality is the primary target for the use of that information. Between data exchange and PHRs, the idea that medical records are static, paperbound entities is rapidly becoming inaccurate. There will in fact be paper records for at least a another decade or two, as the older records gradually age out of the retention timeframes so that they may be destroyed, but those timeframes can range from seven to 30 years dependent upon state, federal, and other rules, regulations, statutes, and typical practices. Therefore, any LHR planning must encompass the newly evolving electronic record, the PHR, and older paper environment for the foreseeable future.

Preparing for common LHR definitions and methodologies across not only the physician and hospital provider organizations but also data exchanges such as RHIOs, the NHIN, and PHRs will require continued focus on the legal processes that surround the records from each of these entities and applying these more common concepts across the new venues from where the records originate. Here we explore the more common areas among these varying record sources and discuss methodologies that are typical across them all rather than their deeper differences.

In this book we address the rather nebulous subject, commonly referred to as legal health records or as they are sometimes referred to, legal medical records. There are few, if any, incidences where any type of legal records are called out by name within EHR standards. The net result of this failure to define legal health record is that there is not a standard terminology for these records and the wide audience of record users and creators do not understand exactly what is meant by the term legal health record. However, since there are an increasing number of parties actually working on what they (and the media) refer to as the legal health record, this term is becoming *de facto* acceptable parlance in the healthcare industry, even without a real standards-based definition. Given that there is legitimacy in the *concept* of legal health records, we will illustrate and clarify these concepts, along with describing the best practices commonly found on the subject from an introductory perspective. There are other publications that explore these concepts in greater depth. This book, however, is intended to define the foundations and preliminary elements for the reader in a fashion that creates a good starting point for understanding the issues surrounding legal health records.

Many associated with the healthcare industry believe that the well-recognized, so-called *primary* uses of health information—including the documentation of care at the point of care and the provision of patient histories for care delivery—are almost exclusively the driving forces for creating and maintaining health (medical) records.

This tends to be the point of view of the providers of care, one that is not incorrect but is somewhat limited in scope. There is in reality a much wider scope and reasons for creating and maintaining sound medical records. Medical records have many uses as *secondary* health information for not only continued treatment but also payment, operations, and compliance with myriad rules, regulations, and laws that guide healthcare delivery in the United States. Other common uses for secondary health information are back-office or administrative uses. These secondary uses are equally as important as the primary usage in the delivery of care.

Although not as glamorous, the secondary uses of health information must be given credence, or organizational efficiencies will suffer, costs will rise, billings will decrease, and liabilities and penalties will increase dramatically. Other examples of secondary health information use, which illustrate why these uses are so important, include medico-legal activities; measuring healthcare quality; and administrative, government, marketing, and research purposes. In addition, they include the necessity for private physicians and hospitals to query and report quality measures; public health agencies to monitor and detect population health indices; the Food and Drug Administration's ability to conduct post-marketing surveillance of pharmaceutical companies; resource allocations by insurance companies; and use of clinical data for comparative effective research by academia. Chart completion, release of information, coding, abstracting, and other familiar HIM processes are considered secondary uses of health information as well.

Medico-legal uses for medical records are often referred to as legal health records, creating a commonly applied concept of record management where the legal system's use of medical records intersects with its other secondary uses. These medico-legal purposes for health information are clearly a significant part of the overarching concept of secondary health information use.

Many of the secondary uses of health information are managed by HIM, registration, patient accounts, information technology (IT), risk management, quality management, and compliance staff. Because these secondary or back-office functions are sometimes deemed less important than the primary use of health information for patient care delivery, the focus at times shifts from the secondary uses and management of the health information in favor of the primary uses. This lack of focus should be avoided by healthcare providers in order to balance the requirements of all health information (or medical record) users, and to maintain fiscal well-being and organizational stability.

These secondary health information data uses may simply be referred to as operations, which follows the model established within the **Health Insurance Portability and Accountability Act of 1996** (HIPAA) for treatment, payment, and operations (TPO).

However named, the concepts surrounding LHRs are crucial to mitigating risks and liabilities as well as helping to provide the most defensible use of medical records within court or other legal proceedings. Remember, any type of litigation could cost a healthcare organization thousands to millions of dollars and is best prevented, especially in today's highly litigious society.

There have been objections to the term legal health records in that it might indicate that some records are more legal or useable in litigation. This is not the intended meaning of the term. Nearly all healthcare (medical) records and related electronic data (except those that are privileged or otherwise excluded) is admissible into **evidence** in court, if they are kept within widely accepted legal practice standards and are thereby considered legal. Rather, the term legal health record is related to a larger conceptual framework. Great care has been taken within this text to avoid confusion and to clarify the use of the word legal to include precise definitions such as the *legal health record defined for disclosure* as opposed to simply naming the concepts *legal records*. Watch carefully for the use of the exact term *legal record*. It is a bit misleading and should be avoided, whether in this text or within the healthcare industry. Modifiers such as "for disclosure" create a more accurate view of the definition and concept. Wherever in this text you see *legal health record* or *LHR,* be aware that it is describing the concept surrounding the medical record defined for disclosure or its accompanying attributes, and not its legal admissibility.

The concepts surrounding LHRs have been coalescing for a period of years and will continue into the foreseeable future. Given the complexity of the electronic health record *and* legal environments, decisions, laws, rules, and precedence will continue to refine the concepts and tenets of this subject. These are not static environments. Be aware of and track the pertinent changes on a continual basis.

The author and reviewers of this text have utilized the most current references available, combined with years of cumulative experience on these subjects. The entire healthcare and electronic record fields are changing at a very rapid pace, especially for legal processes, which in the past have tended to move slowly and conservatively (and in many or most cases still do). This causes uncertainty and a lack of precedence means new case law is waiting to been established. This text is written understanding and accounting for that environment and is derived from common legal principles with their real-world applications in this changing environment.

The most common legal processes across the entire United States and usually the most coherent for our purposes are the federal rules, laws, decisions, and guidance issued by the U.S. Supreme Court, especially in reference to **e-Discovery** (the discovery of electronic records for legal proceedings). There are also two bodies of work from the National Conference of Commissioners on Uniform State Laws (Uniform Commissioners), from which state laws and rules may be derived, that are very similar to the **Federal Rules of Civil Procedure (FRCP)** for rules of both civil procedure and evidence. Federal courts are the venue for HIPAA and Centers for Medicare and Medicaid Services (CMS) compliance, as well as many other legal actions. Therefore, utilizing these rules, as well as those from the Uniform Commissioners, as a basis for information provides useful and sound practice that can be followed by all U.S. healthcare providers, data exchanges, and PHRs. State laws and rules—which are certainly important to many, if not most, legal actions—are so widely variable that no single book can account for all of them. Be sure to research your own state laws and rules for subpoenas, court orders, discovery, and similar legal processes. In no way is this work intended to provide a replacement for the advice from your attorney of legal counsel. We highly recommend that you vet all LHR strategies, policies, and procedures with your legal counsel for his or her advice and any appropriate privileges.

Chapter 2

Setting the Stage for Legal Health Records

Learning Points

- Describe the functions of a medical record
- List departments that have a stake in defining and maintaining legal health records
- Describe why an LHR definition project can be a enterprise-wide strategy for effective management
- Describe what records may comprise a LHR in addition to point-of-service medical records
- Understand that EMR systems must provide legal protections to the organization
- Understand the need to manage overarching source systems for legal purposes

Perhaps one of the most important concepts to remember during the discussion of medical records, or HIM, from a legal system standpoint and other perspectives, is that formal medical record management is actually enterprise-wide in nature as opposed to solely departmental. Decades ago, medical record management was thought of as departmental in nature and the purview of specialists who may have been called librarians or managers. These professionals managed paper medical records and strove for a long period of time for respect and recognition that their roles and capabilities were greater than they were typically given credit for. The principles of record management have not changed, however.

In the 1980s, **electronic medical records (EMRs)** began to emerge as technology and became more oriented to relational databases and personal computers. In the early

1990s, a combination of studies from the Institute of Medicine (IOM) and technological advances began to speed up development and adoption of clinically-based medical records for providers of care. Simultaneously, **electronic document management systems (EDMS)** began to make inroads in the management of scanned and, to a limited extent, interfaced documents contained within medical records, creating systems that the medical record department could manage. In leading-edge hospitals, managers of the clinical systems that dealt with point-of-care records (a *primary use* of health information) simply printed documents and sent them to the medical record department to be scanned and managed separately from the clinical systems that created them. But the vast majority of healthcare facilities still maintained mostly handwritten, paper records at both the point of care and all the back-office areas, such as the medial records department.

However, these small steps forward toward the computer-based records envisioned by the IOM (Institute of Medicine) were not unnoticed by the American Health Information Management Association (AHIMA), which changed the name, face, and mission of the organization and its affiliated professionals from a paper medical record orientation toward the much wider universe of the *information* contained in the records. This proved to be a seminal event. Once the limitations of paper records were removed, not only credentialed HIM professionals but many others in healthcare began to recognize that the principles of record management applied across the continuum of both paper and electronic medical records.

No matter whether they are purely paper, purely electronic, or a hybrid mixture of multiple record formats, the basic principles of record management have not changed. Having a basis in statutes, regulations such as the **Federal Rules of Evidence** (FRE) and FRCP, Medicare regulations, HIPAA, and various state requirements, record management in general remains the same as it has been for decades. What *has* changed is there has been a vast expansion of the specific requirements related to electronic records over that of paper records. The underlying principles remain constant, but their execution in best practices has changed as illustrated in the FRCP rule summary provided in chapter 7.

Carefully strategized, organized, and efficient work processes providing high-quality record keeping are still a requirement for healthcare providers. Now, however, the requirements for managing all the disparate components of information that comprise the dozens of types of **data** that come together to form medical records takes these core principles to new depths of complexity. The same basic concepts remain unchanged, but the scope and depth to which they must be utilized in daily operations are indeed expanded.

Examine the functions of record management espoused by AHIMA, and you will see that none of the principles of record management change with the introduction of electronic record systems. The fundamental principles of managing medical records remain the same whether their format is paper, electronic, or hybrid.

AHIMA, in multiple publications, defines the functions of a medical record as:

- Supporting and documenting decisions made for patient care
- Supporting revenue cycle processes
- Serving as a legal business record for care providers

The work performed by back-office stakeholders in relation to HIM impacts everyone who uses medical records, just as the data contained within the various EHR systems will not be used exclusively by providers of care at the point of care. Providers of care and back-office information managers *both* are equally important in the healthcare delivery equation. Both represent enterprise roles, not just departmental, compartmentalized, limited-scope functions. In order to maximize patient safety and satisfaction, control costs, and reduce liabilities, all members of the healthcare team must work together. This is especially true for how medical records interact with the legal system. Now, record management focuses on back-office record management and also addresses key processes, such as how medical records are created, documented, and used for patient care. These processes are part of the overall requirements for record management that produces eminently defensible records for legal use.

Keeping this in mind, it is easier to understand that the LHR is a function of the EHR that must contain appropriate tools (such as software applications) for its management. The HIM professional's traditional role of managing a more department-based paper medical record is quickly expanding in many organizations to include management of the associated information and to support processes throughout the many and varied EHR systems being deployed. HIM professionals not only work in their traditional roles (i.e., the HIM department), but their information management skills today are used in more expanded roles in healthcare provider organizations such as informaticists in IT departments, database managers, IT system analysts, privacy officers, etc.

Stakeholders for Legal Health Record Definition Projects

The stakeholders in any LHR definition project and the processes that surround both the legal and healthcare processes that manage these records are an enterprise-wide, diverse group. Any LHR definition project should include stakeholders from as many levels of the organization as possible. One word of caution: be careful with your project member selection, as champions of your efforts will yield much more productive work than naysayers. While all opinions are welcome, be sure to vet your prospective stakeholders to ensure that they have the organization's best interest and not some parochial sub-view at heart. See Chapter 3 for more information on project champions and a list of common stakeholders. Recommended stakeholders are listed in figure 2.1.

Whether all of these parties attend each meeting or are called upon as necessary is a facility decision. However, recognize that all these stakeholders can play key roles in defining strategies and making them operational as the tactics will be vetted and readied for rollout within the organization.

Legal Health Records as an Organizational Strategy

So many changes are being fostered with the hyper-accelerated movements toward EHRs, in both the ambulatory physician and hospital environments, that there is a preponderance of challenges to overcome as the systems are implemented. Typically, both healthcare and the legal professionals have been slow to adopt changes, but ARRA incentive funding for adoption of certified EHRs is pushing the boundaries of the traditional behavior of both of these professions. Changes are occurring at such a pace that all parties are struggling to keep up.

Topics like LHR definitions and the discovery processes surrounding electronic records are being foisted upon even the usually reticent parties like technology-resistant physicians, attorneys, and many different venues of court judges. Hospital and practice administrators, chief information officers (CIOs) and even traditional HIM professionals are racing to find the time and resources to manage clinical implementation and qualify for the incentive funds associated with meaningful use, along with limiting their legal liabilities. All of these changes are spurring organizational strategies to facilitate the changes necessary to keep pace with the migration toward increasingly electronic records.

LHR definition projects, once rare and only being accomplished at more leading-edge facilities are now common at many hospitals and physician practices, as well as other venues of care such as ambulatory, long-term care, and hospice settings. When regulatory changes such as HIPAA expansion and security audits, recovery audit contractor (RAC) evaluations, and fraud and abuse audits are factored in, organizational strategies tend to be examined in detail. Organizations with exclusive, singular areas of focus—such as concentrating on the provider of care to the exclusion of back-office processes—are being forced to change to keep up with current industry requirements. This trend is going to continue for years, as the migration toward increasingly electronic records is so complex that long timeframes for full adoption are mandatory.

Figure 2.1. Recommended stakeholders

'C' suite and practice managers. In general, the more supporting 'C' Suite (chief executive officer, chief operating officer, chief information officer, and others) and practice manager-type stakeholders bought into the project the better as they will support development of project materials and strategies that must be institutionalized. They may not be present at all meetings, but they must be involved enough to help determine strategies, sign off on them, and help make them operational. There are good reasons to have some powerful stakeholders to get the respect and attention these projects require.

Clinicians (including physicians, nurses, and ancillary clinical staff) and other staff that develop, create, input, modify, update, and use the data contained inside EHR systems as part of their daily practice bring unique and vital information to the project team. Clinical informatics professionals, especially nursing clinical informaticists, are extremely valuable in guiding legal aspects of documentation procedures that factor into LHR definition and organization projects.

HIM professionals should lead the LHR definition project as much possible. This increases their organizational stature and presence in important clinical EHR decisions. The strategies decided upon are typically carried out in large part by HIM staff, who ensure the accessibility, completeness, accuracy, reliability, and archiving of the EHR and paper-based medical record information. HIM staff also typically manages the subpoena disclosure and release-of-information processes for medical records.

Information technology staff, from the CIO to HIM and EHR analysts, also have key roles. Management and direct custodians of the various EHR and source systems that feed the EHRs are absolutely crucial to the success of a LHR project. IT staff are responsible for the hardware and software applications that manage electronic records contained within EHR systems. They have invaluable information about the granular level of details on how the software should operate and how it is implemented to work within the organization.

Legal counsel (internal and/or external) and risk managers both play roles in subpoena disclosure, litigation response, and discovery (or e-discovery) processes. Vetting of LHR policies and procedures is also required.

Privacy, compliance, and security officers; risk managers; and quality managers all have key roles to play in these projects in that the decisions arrived at directly affect their daily work processes. Risk managers are many times an important HIM ally in LHR definition projects as they understand the liabilities and embrace strategies to reduce them.

Record custodians from patient accounts, diagnostic imaging, and physician practice areas, along with secondary custodians such as source system (for example, laboratory, radiology, and transcription) managers, are also valuable to the project. Record or data stewards are titles also related to record custodians; however, their scope of responsibility may be somewhat wider than record custodians.

Consultants and many HIM professionals are being empowered to work with IT and their organizations to define, organize, and strategize about the roles each stakeholder and their respective workgroups or departments play in the overall delivery of care. In general, this is good news. There must be continued focus on the development of strategies that reduce legal liabilities and risks, which thereby shrink the overall cost of care.

LHR projects are organizational strategies because they are increasingly viewed as an integral component of the strategic imperative of successfully designing, building, implementing, and leveraging adoption of electronic health record solutions. Also they require not only that care providers perform their roles in well-defined ways—such as adhering to timely, accurate documentation practices that reduce fraud and stand up well in court—but also require them to work with back-office stakeholders to achieve a more unified approach to HIM. For years, HIM as a profession has pushed to get recognition and seats at the table for organizational strategies and planning, especially those surrounding EHR selection and implementation. While not completely there, progress is being made on this front.

ARRA has clearly identified both healthcare informatics and HIM as areas that require significant growth during the transitions to EHRs. This is patently correct and is well demonstrated in the marketplace. Clinicians are very busy people with little extra time and resources, and for them to migrate to electronic systems is tough, as many times such implementation requires almost complete transformations in their practices. It is to be expected that parties such as IT and HIM must be leaders in movements toward strategies such as legal risk reduction, which is exactly what is being seen in the healthcare and legal professions.

This text presents detailed strategies for organizations to employ in determining their LHR definitions and litigation response practices. These strategies have genesis in both legal and record management practices. However, these strategies are weighted toward formal record management processes because they are primarily focused on the record manager audience. However, it is not as if the other healthcare stakeholder's requirements, especially legal professionals, are not addressed. There is, in fact, a great deal of information for all parties who manage and work with medical records, regardless of their format: paper, electronic, or hybrid.

Record-Keeping Categories and History in U.S. Healthcare

Exploring the myriad records found in healthcare, certain generalities regarding record management principles can be discerned. As mentioned in chapter 1, there are business records that address treatment, payment, and operations (TPO) for any healthcare organization. The broadest subdivisions of healthcare records commonly accessed for legal reasons are often referred to as medical, billing, and diagnostic imaging records.

The creation of a medical record may begin before a patient's admission and they are definitely expanded during the patient care episode. These records are routinely kept for all healthcare visits from a physician's office to an inpatient stay or any other type of episode of care. It is a new concept that patient record information—existing in the form of historical records from other providers of care or (the patient created and maintained personal health records or PHRs)—can be added to medical record creation at any time before or after a patient's visit.

Billing and other operational records are also common and kept by healthcare providers. Many of the elements of LHRs discussed here apply to many types of healthcare business records, including billing and operational records. But this text centers around the most complex of these business record sets: the medical record.

Medical records have been kept in an organized fashion in the United States since at least the 1800s. Perhaps some of the earliest U.S. medical records are logs kept on sailors from New England. To think that these handwritten logs, which are still readable today, have been so well maintained is inspiring but also illustrates the significance that has been accorded record management of treatment records. The American Association of Medical Record Librarians (now AHIMA) was formed in 1928 to formally set forth guidance on organizing and managing medical records. Record management progressed dramatically throughout the 1900s and has been evolving at an exponential rate since then. There are now three main types of medical record management: paper, electronic, and hybrid. These record types will persist for decades, but in ever-changing ratios and mixtures.

Paper, Electronic, and Hybrid Medical Records

Paper medical records, which have prevailed for more than a century, are mostly self-evident in their content and practices, and can be easily described, as in chapter 9. Paper records permanently record health information through the use of handwriting, transcription, or printouts. They are stored in paper folders or similar hard copy files, and are maintained in this form until destruction. At some point in their lifecycle, healthcare entities may convert and replace their paper records with archival scanning into electronic document management systems and/or EHR systems at which point the paper record becomes a hybrid record.

There are myriads of federal, state, and other statutes, rules, and regulations (see chapter 9) that guide what must comprise a medical record; however, these have largely been addressed by paper records to date. Electronic records can and should utilize these requirements, combined with current paper medical record documents to help create the legal health record defined for disclosure. Defining electronic medical records in the sense of what is to be disclosed for legal requests is more difficult than defining disclosure from paper records, but when viewed from common record management practices in U.S. healthcare and based upon today's typical medical record components, the definition comes into focus more easily as illustrated within two classifications adapted from concepts of the federal rulemaking about meaningful use of certified EHRs:

1. The record should be totally electronic in permanent management and storage across its entire lifecycle, regardless of whether it was produced initially from paper handwritten notes (and later scanned into a computer-based system) or directly entered via data input into a computer, personal digital assistant, or microprocessor device.
2. The electronic record that is wholly electronic may be housed within a single EHR module (system) or multiple record systems that have centralized viewing capabilities, work together to form a complete EHR, or are comprised of a well thought-out hierarchy of business records that are useable for legal defense.

An electronic healthcare record may be created, managed, and finally destroyed in one computer system or may be compiled from two or more systems that can be referred to as *EHR modules*. Multiple EHR modules make up a *complete EHR*. Again, this assumes a completely electronically-based medical record. This is the desired state for U.S. healthcare records. Achieving true, complete electronic health records is the ultimate goal of many recent laws, rules, and practices.

Hybrid medical records are increasingly seen as the most common transition points between fully paper and completely electronic records. Remember that transitioning from paper to electronic records is costly, very time consuming, and hugely reliant on vendor applications that may not be as well conceived as their users would like for them to be (as is often discovered during system implementation). Hybrid records may be a mixture of paper and electronic or multiple electronic systems that do not communicate well or are not logically architected for record management.

Hybrid records are not usually as effectively and efficiently manageable for legal health record purposes as well-crafted, completely electronic record systems. Sometimes they are even less efficient than original record systems from which they evolved. Why? Because they are, at times, created from a perspective for the providers of care, regardless of the issues they cause HIM as they try to manage a sound and efficient legal health record. This results, in many cases, in inefficient records for record management processes, higher costs, and even, at times, higher liability and reduced ability to serve as a primary tool for legal defense. Typical HIM practice has seen these issues be proven true time and again.

Some names for medical records kept electronically are listed below. See appendix A for the glossary of terms related to the LHR.

- EHR: Electronic health record
- EMR: Electronic medical record
- CPR: Computer-based patient record
- PHR: Personal health record
- LHR: Legal health record

The Role of the Healthcare IT Vendors

The basic concept that EHR systems must manage protective (or defensible) record-keeping systems has been overlooked by many, but not all, software application vendors. At times, these vendors—which develop, deliver, and sometimes maintain the hardware and software comprising the EHR—eschew these types of functionalities in the design and development in favor of systems that are blatantly oriented toward the care provider. Healthcare organizations should exercise caution in evaluating vendor applications to understand how protective and effective the business record-oriented functionalities are expressed within each vendor's product.

Because HIM is a *required* set of processes for all healthcare enterprises, it behooves the organization to employ efficient HIM and business record processes using vendor hardware and software applications that recognize the importance of these tasks. Such applications should include dedicated, specific functionalities to address automation and the EHR system applications that impact the LHR. Additionally, these functionalities must be cataloged during the legal health record definition process as discussed in chapter 3.

The medical **record custodians** also may be known as record stewards; typically the HIM workgroup is commonly charged with leading definition projects for both the medical and legal health record. They are also expected to develop proper organization, management, guidelines, and processes related to the use of business records as a protective legal defense tool. (See chapter 5 for more on record custodians.) Most of the time, this effort is performed in conjunction with other stakeholders, such as IT, compliance, and risk management.

Frequently, record management processes associated with the legal uses of the healthcare record are forgotten or de-emphasized during EHR system selection and implementation. Usually this omission is discovered and resolved over time, through operational recognition of their importance when the lack of efficient record management raises risk within the healthcare organization.

In the past, EHR vendors pushed to design and develop functionalities that they thought would please their customers and increase sales. ARRA and meaningful use criteria for certified EHRs are changing that focus to a more consistent set of requirements. It is also a fact that meaningful use includes record management functions, such as the delivery of electronic copies upon request. With these more consistent ARRA-based demands, the record management elements of all EHR modules will continue to become recognized as increasingly important, which is the desired result. Stakeholders who procure, implement, and operationalize EHRs will tend to examine not only the clinical applications, but other user needs as well. This trend will assist in creating a more favorable, legally-defensible record keeping environment.

Managing Source Systems

It is also important to remember that once fully electronic records are implemented, one of the healthcare organization's main objectives must be to strictly manage both the EHR module-based records from whence the permanent, archival, formal EHR is derived, and any paper records with which they may be combined in a hybrid record state. **Source systems** are EHR modules (or in rare cases complete EHRs) that create documentation, data, and **metadata** that ends up comprising the medical and financial records of a facility. Many times, there can be dozens of source systems such as lab, radiology information system, EKG, and many others. Often these source systems do not manage the final aggregated copies within more global clinical data repositories, but it is important to manage their data as well as that in more aggregated repositories. These source systems are often different record custodians than the primary HIM custodian, that is, the laboratory department head or clinical director may be responsible for this source data. Corresponding record sets contained in separate source software applications must be reconciled and agree at all times with those records kept in a more overarching EHR module used by both providers of care and back-office administrators. Such alignment will eliminate liability introduced by having multiple sets of records, some of which may not be submitted to the common medical record chart completion processes. Note that reconciliation is one of the many responsibilities of workforce members charged with data management, integrity, and quality.

Each record type or source system that contributes to the permanent medical record, however it is defined, should have a clearly designated record custodian(s), as the details of record management could impact legal defensibility. For example, the record custodian is responsible for determining whether paper records that are scanned into an EDMS for permanent archiving should be destroyed as soon as practical after scan capture, thereby eliminating a potential source of conflict with the final, permanent, version of the electronic record.

Chapter 3

Creating A Legal Health Record Definition Project

Learning Points

- Explain why it is important to define the LHR
- List five potential stakeholders in an LHR definition project
- Explain why it is important to have a executive sponsorship for the project
- Explain how project management principles apply to an LHR definition project
- List and describe the steps involved an LHR definition project
- Understand why it is important to educate team members and stakeholders in the LHR definition process

Rather than starting with a great deal of supporting terms, concepts and definitions, this chapter presents useful materials that are accessible without a "deep dive" through the entire book. Supporting information is included in later chapters. The hands-on tools included have been proven useful time and again in the marketplace. Use them to facilitate your own LHR definitions, litigation response processes, and preparations for e-discovery. Remember, it is your responsibility as the record custodian or simply the person in charge of the medical record to address these issues proactively as opposed to reactively when time limitations may limit the potential for defensive use of the records.

Why Define a Legal Health Record?

LHR definitions provide formal recognition of which record sets, components, data, and documents comprise the official business records denoted as medical or health records. These defined LHRs may be in purely paper, electronic, or a hybrid combination. When all medical records were managed within paper, it was very easy to designate which record sets were the defined, official records for use in legal proceedings. In today's complex recordkeeping environment where the business records may be contained in any combination of computer systems as well as paper, it is seldom clear or straightforward which record sets are used primarily for legal purposes. Creating sound LHR definitions clarifies the roles of all records and their uses and sets foundational policy for record management operations. Note that these definitions must be formal and published in-house. However, definitions will change as documents and data migrate from paper or other electronic systems, so they must be continually updated as their constituent record components evolve.

LHR Definition Project Steps

Several high-level activities comprise LHR definition projects. Adequate time should be allocated to define LHR in your organization. (See table 3.1.) The timeframes are generally long, and these projects are typically performed by staff members who are already overburdened and may be responsible for multiple facilities. However, the importance of managing the risks and liabilities require that time is spent defining each organization's LHR. At each step in the process, there are requirements for learning new concepts and in researching how other sites have solved similar problems. Be sure that your project team has access to knowledgeable experts and resources to perform these steps. There is much to consider when creating an organization-wide LHR definition project. The following steps are based upon common and standard best practices. Review each to determine what is applicable to your project.

STEP 1: Determine the LHR stakeholder team.

The stakeholder team will drive the creation and undertake the LHR definition project, and be responsible for its continued maintenance. It is highly recommended the record custodian be in charge or included as a member of the team. Adequate control of records is a primary consideration in managing your LHR. Organize your materials into notebook(s) or an electronically accessible format available to all parties who will need access to it. Determine who will be charged with various segments of the operation and maintenance of LHR-related processes going forward.

In the first steps of undertaking a LHR definition, create a process to move the project along according to formal rules adopted by the enterprise. Creating a definition in a small, physicians practice office is simple enough—stakeholders are all nearby and there may be few of them. But the larger the organization, the more complex the electronic record environment and the harder the LHR definition is to achieve.

Table 3.1. LHR definition project steps

Date Completed	Step	LHR Definition Process
MM/DD/YYYY	**Step 1**	Determine the LHR stakeholder team.
MM/DD/YYYY	**Step 2**	Determine strategy and plan for a LHR definition project. Get executive sponsorship and empowerment.
MM/DD/YYYY	**Step 3**	Gather LHR-related knowledge and investigate your state electronic medical record requirements, including retention. Review other related statutes, rules, and regulations. Gain an understanding of electronic record disclosure and e-discovery principles.
MM/DD/YYYY	**Step 4**	Develop a master source system matrix or list that organizes data related to the various systems that create medical record documents, data, and reports.
MM/DD/YYYY	**Step 5**	Create a document matrix* of LHR component documents, data, and reports, at least at the major record section level.
MM/DD/YYYY	**Step 6**	Assess and catalog EHR systems for their LHR attributes within your organization for e-discovery purposes.
MM/DD/YYYY	**Step 7**	Determine and revise affected policies and procedures, including e-discovery and litigation response. Vet these policies and procedures with your legal counsel.
MM/DD/YYYY	**Step 8**	Determine guidelines for LHR maintenance going forward. Continue to maintain and refine your LHR policies and procedures on an ongoing basis. Establish a process for regular review and revision of processes and procedures related to LHR.
MM/DD/YYYY	**Step 9**	Create a slide presentation for education and training for appropriate workforce members.
MM/DD/YYYY	**Step 10**	Conduct necessary training for appropriate parties who will change, affect, use, or provide critical information for the LHR.

*See chapter 4.

Therefore, using formal project methodology is highly recommended. Once the conceptual support of the project sponsorship is secured through the executive vetting of a LHR project white paper, the next area to examine is to which stakeholders should be involved. LHR definitions are enterprise wide in nature and are not typically the product of a single individual, unless the organization is quite small. Careful review of potential stakeholders will ensure that appropriate parties are selected to work on the project. Champions and supporters of this type of project are important, as they many times push the team toward completion. Project supporters are found through experience with senior members of the organization's administration and medical staff. There is no magical formula for identifying project champions, typically interactions leading up to a LHR definition project illustrate which team members can be counted on for support and cogent advice. It is up to record custodians, and risk and legal staffs to facilitate the project with carefully selected project team members. Common stakeholders listed in figure 3.1 may be tapped for inclusion in a LHR definition project. They may not always be present at every meeting, but may be called upon as needed for their areas of expertise. To the extent possible, a larger, enterprise-wide inclusion of stakeholders will tend to drive more common definitions and policies and procedures (P&Ps) across all organizational business records.

It is important to note that an emerging trend within electronic records management is the role of record (or data) stewards and owners. It is important to identify these roles because with IT systems, HIM no longer physically controls the records or record systems like they do with paper records. The stakeholders for an LHR project may also be the owners or stewards from different business units that have content related to the medical record and the designated record set.

Figure 3.1. Common stakeholders

- Administration—Chief of Operations or Chief of Finances
- Ambulatory office managers
- Ancillary staff leader
- Clinical analysts or informaticists
- Clinicians (physicians and nurses)
- Compliance, security, privacy officers
- Data stewards or source system owners
- HIM director or HIM staff
- Information technology (IT) management
- Legal counsel
- Record custodians (for example, staff from patient accounts, diagnostic imaging, and ambulatory services)
- Risk management
- Registration
- Other knowledgeable resources or consultants

STEP 2: Determine strategy and plan for the LHR definition project, and get executive sponsorship and empowerment.

Get executive and other appropriate sponsorship and empowerment. Determine timelines, stakeholders, and strategies for accomplishing the various required tasks. It is recommended that the project timeline be embedded within the critical path of the organization's overall implementation of an EHR solution. Be sure to determine who will vet this entire process and when.

Project governance and leadership is another important aspect of an LHR project. Often the HIM department primary record custodian manages these processes; other times, risk management, compliance, or legal staff may lead. Regardless of which staff members provide the leadership, it is crucial that LHR definition projects be managed as formal projects until they are completed. This means that senior management must buy into the process with governance formally assigned to the project leader with their full backing. Project governance should be thoroughly defined and be well documented prior to commencement of the project to lend legitimacy and help facilitate the tough decisions that must be made as the definitions are determined.

As with any formal project, timeframes, project scope, objectives, meetings, and communications structure as well as related tasks must be addressed. Working within your mandates from the governing parties, set up the project to be successful by being inclusive, straightforward, and task-driven to accomplish your final objectives. Regularly scheduled meetings and conference calls are important to keep the project moving and on track. Expected timeframes can be from a few weeks to many months or beyond. The larger the organization, the longer these projects can run as their elements are neither simple nor easy to accomplish.

STEP 3: Gather LHR-related knowledge.

First, become familiar with the resources listed within this text, which represent the latest thoughts on LHRs. Reading, education, networking, keeping up with AHIMA resources, and questioning experts are all excellent learning methods. Your mission is to become one of your facilities' experts on legal records. Legal staff members are, of course, valuable personnel who will benefit from your focused expertise in this area. Be sure to understand federal, state, and local record retention requirements; and evidentiary and civil procedure requirements that are applicable to *your organization.*

STEP 4: Develop a master source system matrix.

Regardless of its title, the first deliverable from your LHR definition project should be a master list of all clinical, financial, and administrative EHR systems (referred to as EHR modules under the 2010 Meaningful Use rules) that manage or contribute to your medical record; and patient accounts and diagnostic imaging records, if they are a focus of your project. If you are fortunate enough to already have such a list from your IT department, examine it to confirm that it is current and add any other systems necessary to move your project forward. If you must start from scratch, involve your IT staff, as they manage the hardware platforms and software applications that comprise your EHR systems. (See chapter 4 for matrix examples.)

TIP: Spreadsheet-based lists (also called matrices) have been found to be the most useful format for managing this element of LHR projects. Creating a master LHR workbook with associated worksheets is the way professional consultants set up these tools.

STEP 5: Create a document matrix of LHR components.

Once you have created an EHR source system matrix, the next step is to develop a list of documents, data, and reports that comprise your LHR as defined for disclosure. If there are too many documents, data, and reports to list them all (some facilities have thousands of these items), at least record the major record sections. (See chapter 4 for matrix examples.)

TIP: The document matrix is another worksheet contained within your spreadsheet-based master LHR workbook.

STEP 6: Assess and catalog EHR systems for their LHR attributes.

Next, create evaluation criteria in the form of questions to be posed and a space for recording answers. Such criteria will facilitate your assessment of your EHR systems for their attributes that may be important during e-discovery. The key to this assessment is not just asking the suggested questions but asking everything necessary to ensure you clearly understand the EHR, and its functionalities and limitations related to record management. One question will lead to another. Make sure you record the details and create your related policies accordingly. The movement toward electronic records was not steady or uniform or even standards-based prior to ARRA/HITECH. Various vendors systems have wide differences in their abilities to manage LHR-related functionalities. This makes for a more difficult task of defining the details of each system, but with appropriate IT support, they can be developed and listed. (See chapter 6.)

STEP 7: Determine and revise related policies and procedures.

It is necessary to create new policies and procedures (P & Ps) related to the LHR definition project. There may also be existing P & Ps that will have to be updated, so take care to review any existing P & Ps that may be impacted. This entire exercise is best executed with detailed documentation that is difficult to challenge in court due to its accuracy and thoroughness. Be sure to vet whatever P & Ps you create or update with your legal counsel and use them as tools to help educate your attorneys so they can render informed advice. Different organizations will have different manners of vetting. Sometimes risk management and internal legal counsel are utilized; other times, external counsel is used. Whatever vetting process is chosen, be sure to have one.

TIP: Litigation response and e-discovery subjects should be addressed within these P & Ps.

STEP 8: Determine LHR maintenance plan.

Be sure to include regular reviews and updates of your related P & Ps to keep them concurrent with the latest rules and trends in legal health records. It is also a good idea to utilize your actual P & P documents to train your workforce members, which will allow the P & Ps to be continually vetted against real operations and will keep the staff well informed on subjects such as litigation response, record security settings, and **legal holds** for electronic records. Coordination of all facility record custodians should also be an ongoing objective to provide for a uniform, consistent litigation response and advantageous legal processes.

Ongoing LHR maintenance of your EHR systems is required to reduce exposure from litigation, as the legal environment is fluid and changes constantly. Unlike paper records, the electronic record management world requires keeping pace with new developments. As IT systems increasingly penetrate healthcare provider organizations, the LHR must evolve to stay fully protected. Therefore, as IT projects are added or updated, be sure to document where data is located and how it fits into litigation response, legal hold, and other potential legal responses. Update your source system matrix to include new applications, pertinent data stored therein, and the custodians for each system.

STEPS 9 AND 10: Create a presentation and conduct education and training for appropriate workforce members.

Educate as many staff as possible so they will understand and have guidance in following defined LHR P & Ps. These education sessions include administrative, departmental, nursing, medical, and IT staff. It is crucial to educate not only the project stakeholders but also key members from across the enterprise on the realities and processes used to create highly defensible medical records, regardless of their format.

TIP: Tailor the education to the groups to which you are presenting, and take opportunities to attend clinical (nursing and physician) staff meetings to reach a wide audience.

Chapter 4

Defining the Components of a Legal Health Record

Learning Points

- Recognize that the three main components of the LHR are a list of source systems, a list of documents, data, and reports, and an LHR policy
- Describe two methods for developing a complete list of documents, data, and reports that are a part of the LHR
- List five types of documents, data, and reports that might be included in an LHR
- Recognize that an LHR policy can provide a foundation for workforce training

The LHR that your organization defines for disclosure needs to take into account that the LHR is created by a healthcare facility as its *business record* for documentation of the provision of care, which includes information that will be disclosed upon appropriate legal request. The LHR definition of what is routinely released for an initial disclosure does not really affect later discoverability; given appropriate legal processes, most, if not all, of any EHR's data will be discoverable.

There is a relatively new legal concept called *reasonably accessible* that is used in relation to the legal disclosure of EHR data and documents. The genesis of this concept is the December 2006 amended Federal Rules of Civil Procedure (FRCP), which addresses electronic discovery (e-discovery) processes for electronic records. Healthcare organizations have a responsibility to quickly respond to appropriate legal requests (such as subpoenas or court orders) for medical record disclosure and should build their polices upon a foundation of what is reasonably accessible as well as what is *unreasonably accessible*. During disclosure or e-discovery legal processes, your definitions may be challenged; however, it is prudent to think of these items on the front end of the definition process and modify them, if necessary, as time goes on. It is also of note that costs associated with production for both reasonable and not reasonable e-discovery can be levied by a court, so they should be included in your LHR definition process (Dunn 2007).

Because healthcare providers get to initially define what is reasonably accessible, and given the volume of requests for information faced by the typical HIM department (and other record custodians within the organization), it is wise to catalog and define with policies and procedures (P & Ps) exactly what will be divulged upon the most common types of legal requests. State what is reasonably accessible and customarily provided in these policies. It is also advisable to create catalogs of information that illustrate an understanding of the items that are retained as records or data but that is not to be disclosed upon initial legal request. Plan for and catalog what may be harder or unreasonably accessible as well, although this may not be published for external party consumption.

Real-world healthcare demands efficient, replicable procedures for typical requests for record disclosure. Vetting all legal requests through legal counsel will afford the most protection of record custodians charged with **release of information (ROI)**. However, due to the high volume of these requests, this step is almost never performed in the hospital environment unless some kind of red flag relating to litigation, such as receipt of a subpoena, is raised. But typically at the point of the initial request for disclosure, there is no indication of pending litigation and the request is processed according to normal ROI channels. While it is important to handle requests for disclosure with great care if there is pending or prospective litigation, it is also important to manage routine requests for disclosure with consistent, well-documented procedures. Luckily, HIPAA and formalized ROI rules have created a stable environment in most healthcare provider organizations. Within these organizations, most ROI has been formalized to the point that they are managed with consistent P & Ps, and created in accordance with HIPAA and applicable state law.

One of the goals of any LHR definition project is to ensure that applicable LHR and ROI P & Ps are updated to encompass the challenges introduced by increasingly electronic EHR penetration into the medical record management environment. This text, however, will concentrate on the LHR-related policies and less so on those for ROI. Each ROI policy should be updated to stay in context and synchronize with the LHR definition and supporting materials, such as their P & Ps.

Creating Your Tailored LHR Definition for Disclosure

The best way to define your routinely released (disclosed) LHR documents is to begin by building upon and updating existing paper records, policies, procedures, and principles. Utilize new tools designed to address the specifics of LHR disclosure and e-discovery within EHRs. Before you start, have accessible and review related P & Ps and previous ROIs that will give you background on LHR definition work that has been accomplished in the past. Match these P & Ps with the tools and templates outlined in this chapter.

The first task to be accomplished, after identifying your stakeholders and project structure, is to request a list of all clinical information EHR systems. These may be referred to as clinical EHR modules or source systems (table 4.1). The list should include not just the names of these systems but additional data fields such as the resident system expert, vendor name, data format, and others listed in table 4.1. Formulating and maintaining a list of other organization record custodians and their corresponding record sets is advised. Be sure to delineate who responds to subpoenas and other appropriate legal requests for diagnostic imaging studies (films and images) and patient accounts records, as well as any other records for which there are additional custodians. Adding IT and EHR support staff to these lists is recommended as well.

The next task is to create a list, called a document matrix, of all documents and data that comprise your current LHR utilized for routine disclosure. (See table 4.2.) This may actually be a list or simply point to the master document table within an electronic document management system (EDMS). This typically comprises a list of hundreds of documents and can become unwieldy. Therefore, it is recommended that you create a list of chapters (or sometimes known as index tabs) that are *included* in your paper or hybrid medical record and begin a spreadsheet-based matrix to manage these data. (See table 4.3.) It is a good idea to create a single spreadsheet-based workbook (using Microsoft Excel or a comparable program) and to have these lists of source systems and LHR data and documents on separate worksheets within the workbook.

It is important to bear in mind the reason for creating your document matrix as a part of your LHR definition. The record custodian has the responsibility to not only determine what business records, or components of these records, they will release upon legal request, but also determine which records actually fulfill the content of the record request as stated in the request document.

Table 4.1. Source system matrix

Documents Defined as the LHR			Location of System	HQ Site Name of System	Vendor Application Name	Responsible Department	LHR Custodian	Business Owner/ Source System Custodian	IT Primary Contact	Media and Storage (P) Paper— (E) Electronic	Data Format(s)	Retention Period
Document Name Data Set Report Name	Source System	Comments										

Table 4.2. Document matrix key

	Document Matrix			
	Document Name Data Set Report Name	EHR or Hybrid	Source System	Comments
Definition	Record the names or identification of the document, data, or reports included or excluded within the LHR.	List the EHR system or module contained within the LHR. List the hybrid components contained within the LHR.	The EHR system or module that created the data, document, or report that is utilized within the LHR definition	General comments related to this document.

Typically, a document matrix (such as table 4.3) should be created in a spreadsheet with details about the documents and data *included* in the LHR defined for disclosure. *Excluded* documents and data that are commonly used, or even filed and stored with LHR components should be listed as well (table 4.4). Common documents from your previous or current paper-based medical record are nearly always included; therefore, your paper records are typically a good starting point for populating your matrix. It is recommended that you use a notebook with plastic sleeves to hold paper document samples associated with a spreadsheet-based matrix to catalog the documents and data that are defined as LHR components in order to have them available in an organized manner throughout your project. Electronic folders or project collaborative sites should also be established to assist in cataloging details of data, documents, and source systems.

Your organization may already have completed projects that generated lists of documents that could serve as the basis of your document matrix. Such projects include forms redesign projects, especially for an EDMS or forms-on-demand projects. In other cases, healthcare organizations have found that their HIPAA-designated record set (DRS) may be a useful starting point for their LHR defined for disclosure if they have cataloged the DRS. Check this DRS list of components and documents for concurrence with your LHR defined for disclosure, as they might be very similar. Be cautious however, that the formal definition of the DRS expands well beyond that of the LHR. The DRS applies to any information within a healthcare organization that is used to make a decision about patient care and includes nearly all documentation with any **protected health information** (PHI). This is a much wider set than the LHR defined for disclosure, even though the LHR is a subset of the DRS. Still, the DRS, if already cataloged, may be a great place to derive document and data for your document matrix.

Table 4.3. Document matrix for documents, data, and reports defined as *included* in an LHR (with examples)

Facility Name			
Document Name Data Set Report Name	**EHR or Hybrid**	**Source System**	**Comments**
Approved for LHR and Routine Disclosure			
Advanced Directives			
Consents			
Emergency Department Report			
Continuity of Care Documents			
Diagnostic Imaging Reports			
EKG & EEG Reports			
Laboratory Reports			
MAR			
Multi-disciplinary Notes			
Nursing Documentation			
Nursing Flow Sheets			
Nursing Graphics			
Operative, Recovery Room, Anesthesia Notes			
CPOE—Orders			
Problem List			
Psychological Assessment Document			
Physician Progress Notes			
Physician Orders			
Transcription			
Patient Billing Documents			
Remits			
Patient ID Photo and Documents			

Use to catalog your documents, data, & reports included in your defined LHR.

Table 4.4. Document matrix for documents, data, and reports defined as *excluded* from an LHR

Facility Name			
Document Name Data Set Report Name	**EHR or Hybrid**	**Source System**	**Comments**
Excluded for LHR and Routine Disclosure			
Administrative Documents, Data, or Reports			
Abbreviation Lists			
Audit Logs			
Coding Query Forms			
Derived Data i.e. Accreditation Reports, Best Practice Guidelines, Clinical Paths, Statistical Reports			
Indexes			
Metadata (that is not otherwise viewable within medical record documentation reports/ printouts)			
Operational Documents, Data, or Reports			
Physician Task Lists			
Privileged Legal Information			
Worksheets			

Use to catalog your documents, data, & reports excluded from your defined LHR.

Included items in your LHR defined for disclosure will include any documents, data, or reports generated in reference to the clinical information types shown in table 4.5. Remember in any healthcare facility there may be multiple versions of these documents, data, or reports for your definition and cataloging. While you want to understand from a macro level where the multiple versions exist and how they are created, for the document matrix you want to limit the list to as few systems as possible, which actually host these data and documents.

Table 4.5. Document matrix for documents, data, and reports *to be defined as included in or excluded from* an LHR according to facility specific decisions and guidelines

Facility Name			
Document Name Data Set Report Name	**EHR or Hybrid**	**Source System**	**Comments**
To Be Determined for LHR and Routine Disclosure			
External or Other Provider Medical Record Copies (that were received & accepted before or during the patient visit)			
External or Other Provider Medical Record Copies (that were received after the patient visit)			
Audio Files			
Diagnostic or Clinical Still Pictures			
E-mail			
Diagnostic Video			
Internal EHR Messaging			
Alerts, Reminders, Pop-up Clinical Reminders			
Personal Health Record			
Portal Documents			
Previous Versions of Documents, Data, and Reports			
Snapshots of Data Within the EHR			
Interface Reconciliation Records			
MPI Merge Records			
Aggregate Data That Contains PHI			
Back-up Data			
Downtime Recovery Paper Documents			
Original Source Files for EHR Data (contained within various EHR modules)			

Use to catalog your documents, data, & reports to be determined for inclusion in your defined LHR

Your objective with this phase of a LHR definition project is to create catalogs or matrices that define what record components are released upon routine legal request, typically as part of your ROI services. It is not necessary to replicate into multiple versions any documents, data, or reports for inclusion in your LHR. Further into the process, the location of the LHR component, whether in a source system or other clinical data repository, matters when you seek attributes of these components that impact the defensibility and legal risks of the records. At this point, however, simply list the components of the LHR you will disclose. Whether copies or originals will be used is assigned in a later step.

Table 4.2 represents an example of a real-world view of how each document, data, or report must be identified not just by name, but also by the system within which it resides as a component of an LHR. Note that this example shows a hybrid EHR where multiple components reside in multiple systems.

Table 4.6 shows which documents, data, and reports represent your LHR defined for disclosure in a summarized view. This summarized view is useful to denote which systems the major record components are contained within, if a longer detailed list is

Table 4.6. Summarized view of LHR components

Facility Name	
Document Name Data Set Report Name	**Comments**
Approved for LHR and Routine Disclosure	
All documents within electronic document management system (EDMS), with exclusion of those listed below:	1. Could be a totally electronic record if the entire LHR is contained within an EDMS. 2. EDMS could be part of a hybrid record system if not all LHR documents defined for disclosure were managed within it.
• Coding queries	Coding queries are contained within EDMS but will not be released as a part of a defined LHR.
• Documents and reports within inpatient EHR system by the following chapters or sections ○ Nursing ○ Progress notes ○ Orders ○ Medical administration records (MAR)	Examples of chapters or sections within a clinical EHR system.
Photographs	There is no way to get an electronic version into our EHR; therefore, this record set is kept in a standalone paper file.

not required. Often this is a good starting point, however, determining and cataloging a deeper, more inclusive view of more documents, data, and reports is recommended so that no record components are missed or fail to be evaluated for the LHR definition. Again, a balance must be struck between evaluating of hundreds of data and document types versus summarizing at such a high level that important details are missed. The depth to which your organization goes to create your LHR definition for disclosure will often be a function of staff capacity, so capture and catalog as much information as you comfortably can.

Creation of both the source system (table 4.1) and document matrices (table 4.3) are related but not identical activities. The source system matrix is higher level and identifies all of the EHR systems involved in the generation of patient information that ends up in a medical record. The document matrix takes this cataloging process a step further by listing the various LHR components—be they documents, data, or reports—and how they are managed, either as fully paper, fully electronic, or in a hybrid record state.

LHR Policy

The process for creating a legal health record defined for disclosure can have many steps, and optimally they should be followed. However, often there is not an exact sequencing of these steps. Another important part of the definition process is to create a master, overarching LHR definition in a policy statement or format. Typically, this policy is created within an organization's defined template and filed in an appropriate filing system, which increasingly is maintained online for all authorized users to access. In fact, all policies should be accessible and readily useable by the entire authorized workforce, the policies should be used as training tools for regularly scheduled review.

Figure 4.1 shows an example of a few sections taken from a well-written LHR policy. This policy was created in conjunction with source system and document matrices.

Figure 4.1. Sections from an LHR policy created in conjunction with source system and document matrices

SCOPE: All organization workforce members.

PURPOSE:

The business record documenting the delivery of healthcare rendered at **<insert site name>** is defined as the *'Legal Health Record'* (otherwise referred to as the LHR). This LHR will be disclosed upon routine legal or administrative record disclosure requests, such as subpoenas. Other routine record (PHI) disclosures will also be based on this defined LHR, such as the subset of the HIPAA defined Designated Record Set for individual inspection, copies, amendment of PHI, and other release of information requests. Minimum necessary provisions under HIPAA will apply to all disclosure requests.

This LHR defined for disclosure is a hybrid record **(if indeed your record is a hybrid, if not modify this language)** created from the paper medical record and **<insert EHR system(s) name(s)>** documents, the two serving together to form the entire LHR Defined for Disclosure.

The scope of this policy is for **<insert site name>** HIM managed records. Other **<insert site name>** medical record types (that is, medical practices and certain other Outpatient Services records) are not currently addressed by this policy.

The Legal Health Record (LHR) at **<insert site name>** includes the documentation of healthcare services provided to an individual in all delivery settings by our clinical and professional staff. The LHR consists of individually identifiable data in any medium, collected, processed, stored, displayed, and directly used in documenting healthcare delivery or health status.

The LHR at **<insert site name>** is a hybrid record **<modify as necessary to reflect your environment>** utilizing both paper-based and electronic documents, which are captured both manually and via electronic processes, see LHR Source Matrix; Document Matrix worksheet, for details of the LHR component documents. Each encounter is maintained under a unit record number and includes subsequent patient visits. Only individuals authorized to do so by hospital and/or medical staff policies and procedures make entries into the LHR. Standardized formats are used for documenting all care, treatment, and services provided to patients.

The LHR contains sufficient information to identify the patient, support the diagnosis, justify the treatment and services, document the course and results of care, and promote the continuity of care among health providers.

The LHR will include records from *other health care providers* as the result of tests and exams when they were utilized for the evaluation of the patient and subsequent treatment.

Figure 4.1. (Continued)

The Federal Rules for Civil Procedure (FRCP) instituted December 1, 2006 expand the process of discovery and provide guidelines for electronic records utilized as evidence and this policy is in accordance with the guidance provided by these rules.

It is important to define the location of the documents (in either paper or **<insert EHR system(s) name(s)>**) within the **<insert site name>** Legal Health Record (LHR) for timely access, use, and disclosure as necessary for patient care and other requirements, such as disclosure requests. As **<insert site name>** transitions from a paper-based record to hybrid records, and then to a more complete EHR, the location and management of the **<insert site name>** LHR must be evaluated, monitored, and kept updated for medico-legal purposes.

The Document Matrix will serve as a dynamic tool used to define the LHR components in their present form. As **<insert site name>** implements new EHR systems, the matrix will be reviewed and updated. It will serve as the guideline for the legal location of our medical record from which we disclose protected health information.

Related Materials:

- Source System Matrix
- Document Matrix

Chapter 5

Litigation Response Policy and Procedures for Record Custodians

Learning Points

- Define litigation response and the typical actions that comprise it
- Explain why written litigation response policies and procedures are important
- Explain what a litigation hold is
- Know why it is important to identify reasonably and unreasonably accessible documents
- Know why it is important to estimate costs of disclosure in advance of a request

The most common meaning of the term **disclosure** in healthcare is the act of releasing, upon proper authorization, copies of business or medical records. Healthcare facilities in general, and hospitals in particular, have such a high volume of requests for disclosure or ROI of medical records that they have formalized policies, procedures, and often dedicated staff or vendors to manage these processes. Other factors contributing to the need for formalized ROI processes are the burdens and liabilities created by HIPAA, and other laws and regulations that apply to health information disclosure. With paper records, these practices have evolved into a stable state over decades of typical practices. The ROI volume is such that healthcare providers will typically manage the vast

Note: This chapter is intended to provide record custodian and related parties guidance on creating commonly applied policies and procedures to be instituted to inform staff and protect records from acts that could cause issues at various stages of litigation. In no way does this guidance proscribe litigation response from a legal counsel's perspective. Those perspectives are applied **in addition to** these guidelines and, as with all other recommendations in this text, only after appropriate vetting from your legal counsel.

majority of all routine requests according to prescribed processes, but exceptions that cause divergence from these normal paths do occur. Healthcare providers must take great care to be able to recognize any release of information request that may become involved in litigation. **Litigation response** is typically the term used to describe the processes that are invoked if the potential for lawsuits or litigation is detected. Litigation response is not only triggered by atypical record disclosure requests but by any sign or action that shows a potential for a lawsuit. Litigation response should result in protective measures being taken to provide maximum defensive posture by the provider, including appropriate responses to subpoenas, court orders, protecting against **spoliation,** the malicious alteration, concealment, or destruction of evidence, or other acts which later can be questioned and even sanctioned by the courts and opposing counsel.

Upon any legal request for disclosure of health information, the appropriate healthcare staff members or contractors will examine the request and determine what is to be disclosed according to predefined policies. A well-defined LHR will assist in appropriately determining exactly which record components are to be disclosed upon routine legal request. However, if the request is in any way unusual or meets the criteria to invoke litigation response as set by each organization, different procedures must immediately be instituted. Staff training and well-written policies and procedures are key to maximizing the use of healthcare business records as tools in legal defense. Litigation response is simply a set of procedures that, when instituted, protects the records—be they medical, billing, administrative, or metadata—from changes that could be viewed in a negative light in later stages of litigation.

Within the FRCP and **Uniform Rules** for e-discovery, once litigation is suspected or known to be occurring, a specific litigation response—including record protections—must be established. These rules apply to federal court, not state courts, but they are appropriate guidance to follow. Because this text cannot address the 50 states and their various laws, rules, and regulations in reference to civil procedure and evidentiary standards, the federal rules will be used to construct recommendations.

Creating Litigation Response Policies and Procedures

Typically, the larger and more complex an organization's healthcare delivery system is, the more likely it is to have formalized P & Ps to set in motion when litigation is known or suspected. But experience has shown that even these organizations may not have codified their litigation response into clearly defined procedures that are used to train staff and ensure that all parties act accordingly. Failure to have well-defined processes can increase liability and financial risk; therefore all healthcare entities from the very largest to the smallest should examine their litigation response policies and procedures to prevent potentially costly lapses during legal actions. Litigation response may or may not be the responsibility of a single department or staff member. In a smaller physicians' practice, where many hats are worn by a few staff, usually the office or practice manager assumes these duties. In hospitals, risk managers, compliance staff, or in-house legal counsel can be responsible for creating litigation response policies and procedures, but health information managers and other record custodians, including IT staff, are important team members, all of whom contribute to the process steps.

TIP: Find and prepare the best person to be deposed who understands your organization's EHR systems, processes, and content rather than prep multiple people on the custodian issues. There is value in having at least one record custodian who understands both the organizational policies and the IT processes.

Development of litigation response policies and procedures starts with documentation of the steps and personnel already performing these tasks, if any. Once the current practices are assessed, formalization into more model processes can occur. The best practices guidelines presented in the next section have been drawn, as has much of this text, from actual practice settings. As always, customize these practices to fit your specifics.

With the evolution to electronic records, it is crucial that risk and compliance managers, legal counsel, and record custodians keep abreast of the evolving federal and state rules related to e-discovery that impact litigation response steps. For example, the FRCP and Uniform Rules for electronic records and e-discovery call for early meetings of parties and clear definition of the e-discovery process at the beginning of litigation. Combining these meetings with discussion of concepts such as whether documents and data are reasonably accessible or **not reasonably accessible** help to dictate the steps to be taken for litigation response.

Litigation Response Best Practices

The steps in figure 5.1 are common to many sophisticated healthcare provider litigation response plans. These best practices are taken from actual experience within healthcare facilities and should be utilized in conjunction with specific plans driven by your legal counsel's advice and details of each legal request and process.

Legal holds are complex and tricky issues that present multiple challenges. Assessment and development of policies defining and managing legal holds are very important for all healthcare organizations. Questions abound as to what data or documents are covered and how to accomplish the legal hold. For example, is a legal hold instituted via an increase in the security level of a patient or encounter within an EHR or is data? Each healthcare organization must decide how to institute legal holds based on their EHR systems and their available functionalities and safeguards, which work to prevent changes or spoliation within each system that manages health information.

Figure 5.1. Litigation response steps

1. Validate the legal notice or source of anticipated litigation.
2. Notify all defined organizational parties.
3. Prepare for discovery—e-Discovery conferences.
4. Identify the records, documents, and data (patient identifiable and non-patient identifiable) types that may be relevant and the product of a discovery/e-discovery process.
    a. Determine which records are reasonably accessible and those that may be not reasonably accessible.
    b. Be prepared to write a document (a report in FRCP terminology) to the court outlining reasons and rationales for deeming documents and data either reasonably accessible or not reasonably accessible, especially where opposing legal counsels cannot come to agreement on what should and can be discovered (or e-discovered).
    c. Understand that protected and privileged information has complex ramifications and should be examined for legal processes that must be managed by legal counsel. Be aware that there are defined (in FRCP, Uniform Rules, state regulations, etc.) processes and concepts surrounding these issues that are beyond the scope of the typical record custodian; be sure to involve your legal counsel in all of these matters, they should take the lead in these areas.
5. Determine what format the records may be produced in.
6. Determine the actual cost structure for atypical, not reasonably accessible disclosure related to discovery. Use **Table 5.3, Not reasonably accessible cost analysis matrix,** to track the cost of these disclosure types.
7. Prepare to allow the requesting party the ability to review, sample, and validate documents or data according to FRCP and Uniform Rule and state discovery guidelines.
8. If determined prudent, a **legal hold** should be placed into effect, whether ordered by the court or not, that identifies and preserves any relevant information, be it patient identifiable or not identifiable, so long as it is potentially relevant to the litigation.
    d. Legal hold steps:
        i. Identify the potential litigation risk (type, source, and credibility).
        ii. The potential risk of information loss if a legal hold is not established.
        iii. Identify all pertinent record custodians.
        iv. Assess levels of knowledge, sources, and locations of relevant information.
        v. Processes by which legal hold notification will be communicated within the organization.
        vi. The timeframe and plan for reviewing the legal hold and when it may be lifted.
        vii. Determine what information is to be placed in the legal hold and how the legal hold will be accomplished.

It is beyond the scope of this text to detail all the mechanisms by which every EHR system could have data or documents secured and held inviolate. Commonly these mechanisms must be determined through the application of legal health record principles and during their definition projects.

Examples of Litigation Hold Forms

The tables 5.1 and 5.2 are taken from actual practice settings and may be utilized to track details of your litigation response plan. Detailing these forms and their surrounding processes is an important step within your legal health record policy and procedure. The concepts of **reasonably accessible** and not reasonably accessible are outlined in chapter 7.

List of Reasonably Accessible Documents and Data

FRCP will require subdividing documents into reasonably and not reasonably accessible lists. Utilize your already-created document matrix to identify which record component data or documents may be easily and readily accessible according to your defined criteria. Create a list that points to major chapters or sections that easily capture metadata within your various hybrid record or EHR modules. Table 5.3 is a sample spreadsheet listing not reasonably accessible data and documents.

Table 5.1. Parties to be notified during litigation response and legal holds

Name/Department	Case	Notice Date	Hold Release Date
Health Information Management			
Risk Management			
Legal Counsel			
Information Systems			
Patient Accounts			
Diagnostic Imaging			

Table 5.2. Mechanisms instituting legal holds and prevention of spoliation

Document name Data Set Report Name	Site Name of System	LHR Custodian	Business Owner/ Source System Custodian	Hold Mechanism	Documents or Data Held
Data Repository					
Portal					
Ambulatory EHR					
Electronic Document Management					
Patient Financial System					
Registration System					
Radiology/RIS					
Radiology/PACS					
Emergency Department					
Fetal Heart Strip Labor and Delivery					
Laboratory					
CPOE					
Pathology Reports					

Table 5.3. Not reasonably accessible cost analysis

Not Reasonably Accessible Document name Data Set Report Name	Site Name of System	LHR Custodian	Business Owner/ Source System Custodian	Resources Required for Retrieval	Notes on Retrieval Mechanism	Cost Factors
Audit log of what changed with document editing	Clinical EHR Module			IT Analyst Database Analyst Consultant Vendor Staff Risk Manager HIM Director Attorney	Complex database searches and reports, creating view of information not provided by product functionality Attorney needed for review for privileged, non-relevant materials	Staff time Vendor fees Consultant fees Copy costs Software tools Opportunity loss for staff Copy costs
Screen view during physician documentation	CPOE			IT Analyst Database Analyst Consultant Vendor Staff Risk Manager HIM Director Attorney	Screen shot capture (snapshots) not available, must re-create screen look and feel with demo program and populate with data derived from audit logs and document versions, very time consuming	Staff time Vendor fees Consultant fees Copy costs Software tools Opportunity loss for staff Copy costs

Strictly speaking, listing not reasonably accessible data or documents may or may not be performed if there is concern that these documents and data could then be more known and available to opposing legal counsel. However, foreknowledge of what data and documents are considered not reasonably accessible is a good idea given that e-discovery meetings and reports must be created and distributed in a very short time-frame once a litigation response process commences.

Costs for Producing Documents and Data for Disclosure

Reasonably accessible data and documents, such as those defined for LHR and release of information disclosure, probably have a mandated, typical, or published fee structure. Not reasonably accessible data and documents that can be found and disclosed upon deeper e-Discovery should, if possible, be cataloged, and estimations or at least mechanisms for how and who would perform these searches should be given thought before an event arises where the court requires sites to execute these tasks. It is recommended to use a spreadsheet to list attributes related to this task, see Table 5.3. Remember, deeper e-Discovery mandates meetings of opposing parties, and advance preparation is always recommended. An adaptation of this spreadsheet may be utilized for responses to the e-Discovery process that become mandated and provided to opposing parties or the court.

An enlightening article entitled "Calculating the Costs of E-Discovery" (Dunn 2007) lists numerous factors that may contribute to the costs of e-discovery, which can, at best, be difficult to estimate. Dunn states that "the cost for discovery may be defined by state law. If not, then a cost analysis should be prepared similar to what was used to define the cost for disclosure to patients after HIPAA was implemented." Costs may include:

- Copying costs (labor and supplies)
- Postage
- Time to prepare summaries
- Staff time
- Consultant time
- Vendor associated costs
- Legal counsel costs
- Opportunity costs (lost opportunities for revenue and staffing during time spent on e-discovery information gathering)

Utilizing the tools already created with source system and document matrices, the following steps can be adopted to assist in cost estimation (Dunn 2007):

1. **Identify all systems that could store patient information,** both patient-identifiable and non-identifiable. Utilize your source system matrix for this step.
2. **Determine how patient-specific data can be extracted** from these locations. Again your source system matrix can be expanded to include cells to capture these details.
3. **Determine the time and other resources** required to extract data from these files that require identification of the appropriate personnel and software resources and the time they will spend on these tasks. Apply labor and supply factors.
4. **Document inventorying effort**. Completely document the initial and ongoing efforts to maintain a current inventory, including the time involved, memoranda used, educational efforts, *et cetera*.

Tips for Sampling

Dunn also states that organizations must also conduct time sampling, best performed in advance of the actual need arising from a court order. Estimating the organization's time and costs must be accomplished to support an appeal. The documentation should provide sufficient detail for each step (labor and resource specific) and any supplies to demonstrate a thorough accounting of time and resources consumed. Consider involving an individual from the cost-accounting department. Use the sample time and resource estimates to project time required to respond to an e-discovery request from an attorney and to demonstrate, if necessary, undue burden or cost.

Chapter 6

EHR System Attributes That Impact Legal Health Record Definitions and e-Discovery

Learning Points

- Explain what an audit log is and why it is important
- Explain what e-signatures are and how they are accomplished
- Describe how business continuity can be maintained during a disaster
- Know what business rules are
- Recognize the dangers of copy, paste, and copy forward
- Recognize the importance of tracking changes to data
- Define metadata and why they are important
- Discuss privacy protections that an EHR should have
- Describe methods to secure EHR data
- Know what spoliation is
- Recognize that EHR systems can impact user workflow

EHR systems, or even versions of the same vendor's system, are computer programs that are developed, implemented, used, and maintained differently from one another. Two identical versions of the same vendor's product can operate and manifest divergent functionalities and workflows. Therefore, it is crucial to understand each of your own EHR systems, how they work in the normal course of daily business, and what can be relied upon from a legal process perspective as their functionality will come into play at many points within litigation or routine legal proceedings. This is especially true as related to questions of their accuracy, trustworthiness, and reliability.

When responding to a legal request relating to EHR, there is not a great deal of time to put together lists of all the important system attributes that create functionalities and user experiences within the combination of EHR (or source) systems that work together to create and manage medical records. Therefore, it is advisable to catalog these attributes in advance during the LHR definition project. If not performed in advance, the cataloging must be performed during the course of litigation. and all answers to specific questions in reference to functionality and system record management attributes should be kept on a permanent basis for future reference.

Given that these attributes should be cataloged, how should a record custodian or other designated information manager undertake the process? This chapter presents a list of attributes and questions drawn from user experience combined with **HL7** record management and evidentiary standards that, when itemized, will provide a deeper understanding of various record management aspects of any EHR. These tools are included on the CD included with this book. Begin with these lists and expand on them to include deeper questions to fully reveal not only how the systems manage documents, data, and reports, but also which are readily and not readily accessible

The following functionalities are important to assess and use in practice, to demonstrate that important, even mandated, attributes are met by your EHR system for optimal defensive legal purposes. It is recommended that these questions be logged into spreadsheets for permanent access and future usage.

Note that many of these EHR attributes are taken from the HL7 record management and evidentiary standards and are an important part of EHR certification criteria, as listed in the ARRA Certification rules.

Once each of these attributes is determined and cataloged, any changes that occur with software versions, product changes, or further implementation, can cause the information to age. It is recommended that you conduct periodic reviews and update these lists to reflect the latest regulations.

Audit Logs

Audit logging refers to metadata kept on each transaction or event that occurs within an EHR system. Not all audit logs are the same. There is wide variability between products and vendors.

1. Audit logs are present within the source system
2. **Data elements** logged
   a. Original authors of medical record information
   b. Dates and timestamps for record creation, modification, view, or deletion of medical record information
   c. Authors of changes in medical record information
   d. Change histories (that is, versions) for medical record information
   e. Alerts, reminders, tasks, other rule triggers

3. Who can access the audit logs?
4. Can audit logs be filtered to easily find needed information?
5. Can audit logs be easily printed?
6. Can audit logs be reproduced onto digital media? If so, which media types?
7. How long are audit data kept?
8. Can reports be run to keep audit log data if it is not permanently stored within the audit logs themselves?
9. Are audit logs routinely reviewed for security violations and discrepancies?
10. Are any of these reviews automated, that is, privacy access reviews; if so what are the details?

Authentication of Entries and Electronic Signatures

How clinical documentation and documents are authenticated or electronically signed can have large ramifications in legal definitions and proceedings.

1. Describe how direct entries are authenticated.
2. What authentication (e-signature) fields are displayed on each entry?
3. Describe the mechanisms utilized for e-signatures attached to documents, data, and reports.
4. Is there a global, "sign all" capability that is utilized within the source system?
5. Is there a second personal identification number (PIN) or password required during the e-signature process?
6. Is there a digitized facsimile of the signatory's handwritten signature attached during the signature process?
7. What are the e-signature mechanisms and how do the e-signatures provide signature **non-repudiation**?
   i. Is there **public key infrastructure (PKI)** or other encryption of the e-signatures?
8. Are there attending, resident, or other multiple e-signature rules?
9. Can documents be edited prior to e-signature?
10. Can previous, unedited versions be viewed on a permanent basis?
11. Who has access to view previous versions of unsigned documents?

Business Continuity

Backups, disaster recovery, and business continuity in the face of failures from routine to catastrophic is important to understand from an LHR perspective.

1. How will business be continued and healthcare provided if power or computer services are interrupted?

2. What are the relevant disaster plans, data, and document access and recovery routines?
3. How, when, and where are back-ups accomplished?
4. How often are back-ups and recoveries tested?
5. Is there full off-site redundancy?
6. Are paper documents used during downtime?
   i. Will paper downtime forms be keyed into system when access is resumed? If so, who will perform the keying?
   ii. Will the downtime forms be scanned into an EDM system?

Business Rules

The rules and triggers that create work lists, workflows, and other automated processes within an EHS should be well documented.

1. What business rules are utilized within the source system that impact record management?
2. Describe the **workflow** (business process management or BPM) capabilities, including rules and triggers.
3. Are there work lists generated by automated processes? If so, how do they work?
4. What are the controls, updates, monitoring capabilities of the workflow, rules, work lists, etc?
5. Is there an ability to see previous versions of rules and workflows that may have been in effect in the past?

Cut, Paste, and Copy Forward

Many times the EHR system may offer certain features for cut, paste, and copy forward. How they are implemented and used by the provider is usually a differentiator.

1. Detail the cut, paste, and copy forward functions available within this source system.
2. How have they been implemented?
3. What metadata is recorded in the audit log for cut, paste, and copy forward functions?
4. Can the original author, time date of each entry, copying author, and content copied, pasted, or cut be identified?
5. How do versions control work with cut, paste, and copy forward in this source system?

Data, Document Management, and Non-repudiation

How is the integrity of each document and data elements ensured? Accuracy, trustworthiness, and reliability are key tests of any EHR. Document and data **non-repudiation** are elements of these tests.

1. Which of the following indices are used for data and documents in the source system?
   a. Author
   b. Owner
   c. Content type
   d. Functional category
   e. Date of submission or content creation
2. What documents, data, and report file formats are used in the source system?
3. Is there a specific name and unique identifier for each document, data set, or report that may be included in the LHR?
4. Is the identity of the record creator, information source, or the owner tracked?
5. Is date and time of receipt or creation tracked?
6. What quality control, reconciliation, or other processes are used to help ensure capture of quality documents, data, and reports?
7. What document editing tools are available and how do they work with documents?
8. Can documents and data be deemed complete from a chart completion perspective and be trusted not to have changed after completion processing? How is this accomplished?
9. If changes are accomplishable after record completion, how are changes tracked, versioned, and audit logged?
10. Is there a record, including the date, of when there was the cut-over from live operations for each document, data, and report?
11. How are amendments, corrected, or augmented data, documents, or records flagged?
12. How are redactions accomplished for documents and discrete data elements? Can PHI be converted to non-PHI with redactions?

Data Permanence and Migration Plans

Planning for the eventual obsolescence of a technology is often not given a high priority, but record managers need to understand how data would be migrated to ensure compliance with the long retention period (years to decades) required for EHR systems.

1. Is it envisioned that the data within the source system will be maintained throughout its entire retention period?
2. If migration to a new EHR module or system were necessary, how would the data be migrated?
   a. What kind of output files and formats would be generated and could the documents, data, and reports realistically be migrated?

Interfaces

Most EHR systems import and export documents and data in some fashion. This section identifies how this is accomplished.

1. List inbound interfaces and their formats (for example, HL7, discrete, document, or other).
2. List outbound interfaces and formats.
3. What are your enterprise interface engines, software applications, and architectures?
4. List the audit and error logs for each interface and who maintains them.
5. Who reconciles the interfaces, and what other quality control mechanisms are utilized for each?
6. Are there native chart editing tools that work with each interface and manage the movement of data, documents, or reports within the source system?

Legal Hold

In the event a legal hold is placed as a part of a litigation response or court order, how will it be accomplished within this EHR system?

1. Can data and documents be held from destruction or alteration pending a legal hold or **preservation order**?
2. How is this accomplished for the source system?

Metadata

Metadata are data about data, and are sometimes very hard to quantify. Litigation is highly dependent upon metadata, and metadata is sure to be an issue in e-discovery. Advanced assessment of these characteristics is important to meet short court clocks.

1. List all reasonably accessible metadata within the source system.
2. What data elements are kept for each system document, data, or report within the database, not necessarily within the audit log? Are the following included?

a. Authors of clinical documentation
b. Date or timestamps for record creation, modification, view, or deletion of clinical documentation
c. Authors of changes in medical record information
d. Change histories (versions) for clinical documentation

Output: Printing

Print management is the most common form of output. In today's meaningful use definition, other forms of electronic copies and similar output are of equal importance.

1. In what format(s) can data be output from the source system?
2. Into what media can output be placed?
3. What kind of data exchange is available?
4. Can the output be encrypted with **HIPAA-grade encryption** to created secured PHI?
5. Can a continuity of care document (CCD) or continuity of care document report (CCR) be output?
6. What data about printing can be captured in a footer or banner?
7. What data in reference to printing is captured in the audit logs?
8. What and where are documents, data, and reports printed?
9. Is there auto-printing or on-demand printing?
10. Is there a distinct printing application? If so, what is its name and how does it operate?

Permanent Storage

LHRs must be able to store information on some kind of permanent basis. What are the details?

1. What storage architecture(s) or system(s) are used for permanent storage of documents, data, and reports within the source system?
2. How are documents, data, and reports stored, and in what format(s)?
3. Can documents, data, or reports be destroyed on a defined retention schedule? If so, what are the mechanisms?
4. Where is physical storage of these documents, data sets, and reports?
5. Is there any kind of hierarchical storage management that impacts storage location or retrieval response time?

Privacy Attributes

Given that HIPAA has strengthened privacy rules and their enforcement has increased, the following EHR system attributes take on elevated importance and matter in determining privacy violations and breach notification.

1. Does the EHR system create secured or unsecured PHI by HIPAA definition?
2. How are patient requests for access, viewing, and copying accomplished for this source system?
3. How are requests for restrictions (out of pocket and other) accomplished?
4. How is **accounting of disclosures** (AOD) tracked?
5. Is the audit log work detailed enough for privacy and access audits?

Rendition

Rendition is the act of rendering data into documents, usually in report form. Report writers are the most common form of rendering, but there are others such as the creation of documents for continuity of care based on pre-programmed routines.

1. By what mechanism are data or reports rendered into documents?
   a. If a report writer is used, is an overlay or other third party used to render documents from data or reports?
   b. What is the product name and version?
2. Who has control over changes to accepted renditions of documents and reports?
3. What process is used to manage changes to standard accepted renditions?
4. How does rendition work with version controls?

Retention

Archival storage of health information is always an important consideration for record managers. How data and documents are retained and then destroyed should be carefully determined and documented.

1. Is there a published retention schedule for all the documents, data sets, and reports in the source system?
2. Is the identified storage location capable of auto-purging records, documents, data, and reports according to a published retention schedule?
3. How will this destruction be managed from a technical perspective?
   a. Is destruction HIPAA compliant for secured PHI?
4. Who manages the destruction?
5. Are purge lists required? If so, from what database?

Security Attributes

Privacy works with security attributes to create secured or unsecured PHI and to meet meaningful use criteria. Security is the domain of the security officer, but record managers need to be familiar with high-level security protocols used within each EHR system.

1. Describe the HIPAA security mechanisms.
   a. Is data encrypted to create secured PHI for data at rest, in motion, and in use?
2. Describe the source system general security model.
3. Are there both user and group concepts?
   a. What permissions can be granted to each user and group?
4. Is access to the system global and logged or defined by locations, role, or other criteria?
5. Is access monitored on a routine basis? If so, provide details.
6. How are security violation complaints managed?
7. Who are designated as administrators and data stewards within each application and source system?
8. Is direct patient access allowed into EHR systems? If so, describe.

Snapshots and Screen Views

So-called snapshots of data or how screens are populated and what they looked like at discrete points in time are increasingly being asked for in legal proceedings, but as yet these are rarely provided in a satisfactory manner within EHR systems. Often, these become not reasonably accessible items, as they are hard or impossible to create due to a lack of capability provided by the vendors.

1. Can snapshots of data at discrete dates and times be captured and preserved?
2. How does this process interact with security and version controls?
3. Are these snapshots noted in the audit long?
4. How long are these snapshots available?
5. How would screens be presented if a court asked for a view of what a user saw at a certain point in time on a screen?

Spoliation

Preventing **spoliation** is of prime importance to preventing court-ordered sanctions and increased legal liabilities. Usually these are combinations of system functions and policies and procedures.

What source system functionalities are used to prevent spoliation?

Version Controls

When changes or new data or documents are added, how are the old versions managed? Are they available or overwritten? Each EHR system typically has its own version management, but also contains flexibility in implementation.

1. Does the source system keep previous document, data, and report versions?
2. Are all versions kept permanently or are there options, especially for incomplete documents that change during chart completion or other documentation processes?
3. Is document viewing a secured permission?
   a. If so, who is allowed to see which versions of documents, data, or reports?
4. Are versions date and time stamped?
5. Do e-signatures trigger new versions?
6. Do annotations trigger new versions?
7. Do amendments trigger new versions?
8. Are old versions of rules, alerts, and triggers maintained?
   a. Can they be associated with dates and times of previous documentation? Is the version of rules, alerts, and triggers that was in effect for previous documentation available?

User Workflow Impact

During the LHR definition process, many times part of the definition entails designating EHR systems to wholly or partially (in the case of hybrid records) manage data or documents in an electronic state. The readiness and impacts of using an EHR system for this purpose needs to be assessed. Use the following questions to assess impacts on your system, whether it is either a hybrid LHR or a fully electronic system.

1. What is the impact on inpatient clinical workflows of managing records entirely within this source system)?
2. What is the impact on medical staff committees, and quality, risk, and other operational area workflows of managing records entirely within this source system?
3. What is the impact on HIM workflows of managing records entirely within this source system?
4. What is the impact on patient accounts workflows of managing records entirely within this source system?
5. What is the impact on registration workflows of managing records entirely within this source system?
6. What is the impact on ambulatory care delivery workflows of managing records entirely within this source system?

Chapter 7

e-Discovery Overview

Learning Points

- State record custodian responsibilities with respect to discovery
- Understand that due to the complexity of the EHR, it is likely that a pretrial conference will be necessary to outline what will be released and how
- Understand what is and what isn't reasonably accessible and that the organization must be able to justify a claim that records are not reasonably accessible
- Understand responsibilities for protecting privacy relating to HIV/AIDS, mental health, and substance abuse records

---

There are two main legal processes for custodians of records to be concerned with in relation to your defined electronic or hybrid LHRs: disclosure and e-discovery. Legal counsel will be concerned with both of these processes as well as more traditional legal process issues, such as waivers, timing, and strategies. **Disclosure** is the output and release upon request of appropriate medical record documents, and **e-discovery** is the process of discovering what parts of the patient's records may be used for litigation or further legal proceedings; it is an opportunity for opposing counsel to obtain *relevant* information. E-discovery is named to reflect an emphasis on electronic records; however paper–electronic hybrids may also be included. E-discovery can be required from a single or a mix of EHR systems and may also require hybrid portions.

The FRCP distinguishes between reasonably accessible records and those that are not. This is the key that allows healthcare providers to define exactly what the defined LHR will consist of that will be released upon typical, appropriate requests.

LHR information, derived from organizations' business records, are admissible into evidence through an exception to the hearsay rule contained within the Federal Rules of Evidence (FRE) (803(6)) and the Uniform Business and Public Records Act, which most states have adopted. The records must be kept in the normal course of daily business, authenticated, and identified prior to admission. The legal and regulatory acceptance of electronic records is predicated on these records meeting certain well-established legal requirements. The basic requirement is that records are authentic and can be deemed to be reliable, trustworthy, and accurate. Tests of these requirements show through various means that the electronic record must have been captured at or near the time of the event or transaction and is complete and available for retrieval.

Amended FRCP amendments took effect December 1, 2006, to more consistently conform to the current LHR environment. These rules are very likely to be adopted by state and local jurisdictions; therefore, adopting them as standards for your facility is prudent. The federal rules continue to mandate formal record *custodianship* as evidenced by the FRCP for electronic records. The record custodian is charged with the ability to certify exact copies of the original record components; supervise all record inspections by third parties; copying or duplicating records for external release for admission into evidence; and attestation to the admissibility, timeliness, and management of the day-to-day record-keeping environment.

Output (printed mostly) can be admitted into evidence if it meets the criteria required by the Uniform Photographic Copies of Business and Public Records as Evidence Act (there are both federal and state versions). This act states that a reproduction made by any process that accurately reproduces or forms a durable medium for reproducing the original is as admissible in evidence as the original itself. Meeting this requirement allows organizations to create and retain LHR data and documents to electronic form, and certainly implies that well-organized and documented record management P & Ps be in place.

The FRCP for e-discovery is responsible for widespread updates and modifications into record management for evidentiary purposes. There are rules addressing legal holds, spoliation, and the e-discovery process, which may take place at the beginning of litigation. Electronic systems must not only securely store data and documents for your defined retention period, but record custodians must also protect them from unauthorized alteration or destruction and be able to secure them from changes during litigation, especially upon court order.

An organization's record custodian also defines the attributes of the LHR and manages its storage, access, release, and retention. The custodian presents the records into evidence when necessary, typically through the use of certified copies of documents. The custodian must attest that the records were kept in the normal course of daily business, and that they are essentially accurate, trustworthy, and reliable. The custodian must always project a credible image in court and during all legal proceedings and should be able to relate key details of the electronic systems that feed and manage the LHR. The sheer complexity of today's EHRs requires record custodians to be able to catalog record management details of each of the EHR component systems. See chapter 4 and the CD for matrices to detail your system components.

The record custodian must work with legal counsel, risk management, and possibly compliance departments to prepare for litigation response in reference to e-discovery and related legal processes. According to the FRCP and Uniform Rules, there is a much greater emphasis placed upon the pre-discovery process where meetings are held (between parties and possibly the judge or officer of the court) to determine what records, data, and documents can and should be accessible or copied for e-discovery processes.

It is also increasingly important to prepare, in advance, experts, including clinicians (nurse and physicians), for depositions by educating and training them for tough questioning, including various facts about print output, screen views, and metadata (that is, date time stamps and audit logs) in order to present credible testimony for legal proceedings. This is a challenge that needs to be well planned and taken very seriously in order to maximize its effectiveness.

E-discovery is not a "fishing expedition" that grants plaintiffs' counsel the ability to comb through all the patient's records looking for issues to litigate. The concept of **any and all records** can be limited in e-discovery—instead, a more focused approach on what is deemed relevant for the case is necessary. Counsels may not agree on these points, and the judge or court officer may be forced to make the determination. Requests stating "any and all records" will be difficult to respond to given the extensive nature of multiple electronic records. If such requests are received, work with your counsel to limit the scope of the request based on relevance to the claim.

Overview of the FRCP and Uniform Rules Impacting E-Discovery and Legal Health Records

The December 2006 FRCP was created by the U.S. Supreme Court and adopted by the U.S. Congress. The Uniform Rules Relating to Discovery of Electronically Stored information were created in August of 2007 and may be adopted by most states. Federal courts require the use of FRCP. State courts have their own rules, but most adopt rules based on the FRCP (or the Uniform Rules). Under all circumstances, thorough knowledge of the federal rules and policies and procedures based on their tenets is advisable. FRCP rules are quite extensive. The most important rules for HIM and IT practice are outlined in this chapter, but all do apply in federal court proceedings.

Discovery during a lawsuit or criminal trial is a process where non-privileged, relevant information can be requested and is divulged. It should be anticipated that initial LHR disclosures are defined by the healthcare organization, but subsequent discovery steps may be undertaken during litigation or other legal processes that will require production of other data, documents, or reports. The new FRCP addresses the discovery process in detail, and the record custodian must be prepared to address detailed discovery requests and arguments in court.

What Is Produced upon Subpoena and What Can Be Discovered or E-Discovered

Remember that LHRs, for all their complexity and depth, have two legal purposes that basically drive and keep the discussion focused:

1. What is produced for evidentiary purposes by your organization's record custodian upon subpoena or other proper legal request
2. What and how potential discovery or e-discovery will be accomplished

This section's focus is on defining these legal purposes and illustrates how healthcare organizations should prepare, institute, and operate ongoing sound LHR processes. Disclosure describes the processes for releasing EHR data to external sources, and e-discovery is the process of legal discovery that takes place within electronic or electronic and paper hybrid records during the various phases of litigation.

Federal Rules of Civil Procedure (FRCP)

The following sections of the FRCP are important to address during your LHR definition and P & P development. Be sure to read the AHIMA Practice Brief from September 2006 entitled "The New Electronic Discovery Civil Rule" for more details. The entire set of rules has been examined for this synopsis.

Rule 16

Pretrial conferences, HIM, and IT should be ready to discuss with hospital counsel the availability of pertinent information and records.

Rule 16(b)

E-discovery processes create a much larger role for the judge than other discovery processes. HIM and IT must be ready to work with legal counsel with respect to issues of retention, storage, type of data in each system, privacy related to HIV/AIDS status, and other PHI.

Rule 26

This rule defines obligations to maintain and disclose relevant records.

Rule 26(b)(1)

This subsection limits the scope of discovery to relevant materials. HIM must help ensure only materials relevant to the action are disclosed despite, an any and all statement that may be specified in the original legal request.

Rule 26(b)(2)

This subsection provides that a responding party does not have to provide electronically stored information that is *not reasonably accessible*. The responding party has the burden to show why the material is not reasonably accessible and still may have to produce the records if the plaintiff shows good cause. However, facilities can require payment for costs incurred as a result of e-discovery. HIM and IT must have specified *in advance* what records or portions thereof are reasonably accessible and what items are not reasonably accessible.

Rule 26(b)(2)(C)

This subsection contains more information about balancing the needs of e-discovery against what is not reasonably accessible. HIM and IT may need to summarize what information is not reasonably accessible and why, as well as what is relevant or not relevant.

Rule 26(b)(5)

This subsection addresses inadvertent or mistaken production of records that were not requested or relevant to the request. Mental health, HIV/AIDS, and substance abuse records may also have provisions related to inadvertent production.

Rule 26(f)

This subsection outlines the necessary discussion between parties for preservation and production of relevant materials.

Rule 26(f)(3) and Form 35

Parties are directed to have early discussions about e-discovery of relevant information and to report on the e-discovery plan to the court. HIM will be responsible for producing the information required in Form 35. Data formats and data relevancy, among other items, are addressed at this time.

Rule 26(f)(4)

Parties are required to ameliorate costs and production delays to avoid waiving privilege or work product production during discovery through agreements that allow for assertion of privilege or work product production after documents of electronically stored information have been produced. P & Ps about what is privileged and what work products are included in the LHR need to be created *in advance*. The P & P should also address how the organization will respond to records with subject material with added protections such as HIV/AIDS, mental health, and substance abuse. This rule also calls for P & Ps to define exact costs and burdens on producing electronically stored information.

Rule 33

This rule defines procedures to answer **interrogatories**, which are written questions to opposing parties in litigation. HIM must be familiar with key EHR workings to be able to provide these answers.

Rule 33(d)

This rule allows electronically stored information to be provided as part of interrogatories.

Rule 34

This rule outlines production of electronically stored documents and provides for occasional testing of documents and electronically stored information. Again, it behooves HIM to understand the technology behind the electronic data and to document record storage and creation.

Rule 34(a)

Production of electronically stored and traditionally stored paper documents stand on equal footing. P & Ps should be periodically reviewed to ensure access and production for disclosure of electronically stored documents. These P & Ps should be periodically reviewed and updated.

Rule 34(b)

This subsection relates to production of documents and being aware of the requesting party's requirements relative to document production. P & Ps should be established defining how designated business record data, including native file format and metadata are to be produced.

Rule 37

This rule addresses failure to disclose issues (absent good faith activities) and sanctions available for failing to produce electronically stored information.

Rule 37(f)

This subsection sanctions **safe harbors** and certain types of loss of information as a result of good faith operations. Good faith operations may include the imposition of a legal hold to prevent data loss; therefore, P & Ps must be clear on how legal holds—and other forms of record safekeeping, as typified HIM processes—will be accomplished and who will be notified.

Uniform Rules

The FRCP rules are directly applicable to federal court cases (that is, HIPAA and CMS related cases are typically held within the federal venue). They do not carry the same force within the various state court venues. However, it is expected that they will be implemented by the states via many routes, such as precedent and indirect adoption.

However, a more direct route for state adoption comes from the National Conference of Commissioners on Uniform State Laws. This group, which met for the 160th year in 2007, creates rules for varied legal situations and processes that are commonly formally adopted by most states. The most interesting point of these rules is that they do not reinvent the wheel, rather, they adopt the 2006 FRCP e-discovery rules, verbatim in most respects. Therefore, learning and using FRCP and the Uniform Rules together virtually guarantee safe record-keeping practices.

The Uniform Rules 2007 overview relating to e-discovery of electronically stored information explains the differences in electronically stored and paper-based information.

> Electronically stored information may exist in dynamic databases that do not correspond to hard copy materials. Electronic information, unlike words on paper, is dynamic. The ordinary operation of computers—including the simple act of turning a computer on and off or accessing a particular file—can alter or destroy electronically

> stored information, and computer systems automatically discard or overwrite as a part of their routine operation. Computers often automatically create information without the operator's direction or awareness, a feature with no direct counterpart in hard copy materials. Electronically stored information may be deleted yet continue to exist in the system, but in forms that may be difficult to locate, retrieve, or search. Electronic data, unlike paper, may be incomprehensible when separated from the system that created it. The distinctive features of e-discovery often increase the expense and burden of discovery.

A summary of the Uniform Rules Relating to Discovery of Electronically Stored information is listed in the following section.

Rule 1: Definitions

- Discovery is the process of providing information in *civil proceedings*.
- Other important definitions listed

Rule 2: Supplemental Rules of Discovery

- Unless *displaced by a particular rule,* rules of discovery already in place are supplemented by these new rules.

Rule 3: Conference, Plan, and Report to the Court

This is an excellent summation of the e-discovery phase of a litigation response plan. This text recommends creation of a litigation response and e-discovery policy that mirrors the following steps as a matter of routine for involved civil proceedings.

- Not later than 21 days after each responding party first appears in a civil proceeding all parties that have appeared in the proceeding shall confer concerning whether discovery of electronically stored information is reasonably likely to be sought in the proceeding, and if so the parties shall discuss:
    - Any issues related to the preservation of discoverable information
    - The form in which each type of information will be produced
    - The period within which the information will be produced
    - The method for asserting or preserving claims of privilege or of protection of the information as trial preparation materials, including whether such claims may be asserted after production
    - The method for asserting or preserving confidentiality and proprietary status of information relating to a party or person not a party to the proceeding
    - Whether allocation among parties of the expense of production is appropriate
    - Any other issue relating to the discovery of electronically stored information

- If discovery of electronically stored information is reasonably likely to be sought in the proceeding, the parties shall:
  - Develop a proposed plan relating to discovery of the information; and
  - Not later than 14 days after the conference under subsection (a), submit to the court a written report that summarizes the plan and states the position of each party as to any issue about which they are unable to agree.

Rule 4: Order Governing Discovery

This rule revolves around the order for discovery a court may impose. It specially lists the following items:

- Whether discovery is reasonably likely to be sought
- Preservation of information
- Timeframe for production and disclosure
- Permissible scope of discovery
- Method of asserting or preserving claims of privilege
- Method for asserting confidentiality and proprietary status of information
- Allocation of expense of production
- Any other issue related to discovery

Rule 5: Limitation of Sanctions

This rule limits sanctions except for exceptional circumstances for failure to provide electronically stored information lost as a result of routine, good faith operation of an electronic information system.

Rule 6: Request for Production

In a civil proceeding, a party may serve another for production of electronically stored information and for permission to inspect, copy, test, or sample the information. Rules for the request and the required response are listed.

Rule 7: Form of Production

This rule allows record custodians to create a default rule (see Table 4.3) for the form that production and disclosure of electronically stored information will take. For example, you may choose to produce paper document copies from a document management system instead of copies from a clinical order entry system.

- A party requesting information may request the form in which it may be produced.

- If the responding party objects to the form requested or there is no form requested they shall list in the response the form intended for delivery to meet the request.
- Unless the parties agree or the Court orders otherwise; if the request does not specify a form for production the responding party shall produce the electronically stored information in the form which it is ordinarily maintained or is reasonably usable.
- A party need *not* produce the same electronically stored information in more than one form.

The final bullet above is a key. Unless there is a relevant reason, there is no need to produce the same information from myriad electronic systems. Certainly in cases where there is dispute over the details of the information stored—be it direct data or metadata—the court could order differing copies be produced of the same data, but in general, courts frown upon receiving multiple copies.

Rule 8: Limitations on Discovery

This rule is designed to address the unique issues raised by difficulties in locating, retrieving, and providing discovery of electronically stored information. Reasonably accessible and cost allocation concepts are also covered.

Rule 9: Claim of Privilege or Protection After Production

This rule discusses claims of privilege and the handling of privileged information.

Rule 10: Subpoena for Production

Subpoenas are used to request information production but reasonable steps must be taken to avoid undue burden or expense.

Rules 11–13: Housekeeping Rules, Effective Date, Repealed Rules, and Uniformity of Application and Construction

Check with your legal counsel to determine whether you are also subject to the Sarbanes-Oxley Act of 2002, which applies to non-tax exempt healthcare organizations and contains electronic record requirements. Many, if not most healthcare providers (hospitals especially) are not covered by these regulations. However, it is always wise to be as compliant to these global rule and regulation sets as possible. This book does not detail this set of regulations.

Chapter 8

Key Legal Concepts

Learning Points

- Know which federal rules apply to the LHR and their general requirements
- Know the different types of subpoena power and what they entail
- Know that patients must be notified when their records are subpoenaed
- Recognize that general subpoena power typically does not cover substance abuse or mental health records
- Recognize that pediatric records are given special treatment under subpoena power

The first step in determining the content of an LHR is to determine what statutes, regulations, rules, policies, guidelines, and standards contain requirements affecting the release of health records and the documentation to be maintained as part of the medical record.

Federal Rules of Evidence

The Federal Rules of Evidence (FRE) specify the types of information that can be permissibly introduced as evidence in litigation in federal courts. Accordingly, the FRE informs the method by which providers must create and maintain their LHRs so the information contained therein can be used in litigation when the need arises. In general, the FRE, through the hearsay rule, prohibits the introduction of evidence that is not a statement by a witness testifying in court. Article VIII, Rule 803(6) of the FRE, however, states that records of regularly conducted activity will be allowed into evidence as an exception to the hearsay rule. Records of regularly conducted activity are defined as shown in figure 8.1.

Figure 8.1. Records of regularly conducted activity

Records of regularly conducted activity are:

> . . . a memorandum, report, record, or data compilation, in any form, of acts, events, conditions, opinions, or diagnoses, made at or near the time by, or from information transmitted by, a person with knowledge, if kept in the course of a regularly conducted business activity, and if it was the regular practice of that business activity to make the memorandum, report, record, or data compilation, all as shown by the testimony of the custodian or other qualified witness, or by certification that complies with Rule 902(11), Rule 902(12), or a statute permitting certification, unless the source of information or the method or circumstances of preparation indicate lack of trustworthiness. The term 'business' as used in this paragraph includes business, institution, association, profession, occupation, and calling of every kind, whether or not conducted for profit.

Additionally, Rule 902(11) states:

> . . . the original or a duplicate of a domestic record of regularly conducted activity that would be admissible under Rule 803(6), if accompanied by a written declaration of its custodian or other qualified person, in a manner complying with any Act of Congress or rule prescribed by the Supreme Court pursuant to statutory authority, certifying that the record:
>
> (A) was made at or near the time of the occurrence of the matters set forth by, or from information transmitted by, a person with knowledge of those matters;
>
> (B) was kept in the course of the regularly conducted activity; and
>
> (C) was made by the regularly conducted activity as a regular practice.
>
> A party intending to offer a record into evidence under this rule must provide written notice of that intention to all adverse parties, and must make the record and declaration available for inspection, sufficiently in advance of their offer into evidence to provide an adverse party with a fair opportunity to challenge them.

Source: FRE, Article VIII, Rule 803(6).

This business record definition sets the basic foundation for determining when a particular document or data element is to be included in the definition of the content of the LHR. For example, a note written by a patient's family member would not qualify as a document "kept in the course of a regularly conducted business activity," so it would not be included in the content definition for the LHR, nor would audit trails related to such correspondence. Although it may not be considered a part of the LHR, if the attorneys determine a note exists, they can request that it be reproduced. Chapter 3 examines how the FRE definition may influence the decision of whether to include documents from other providers, patients, or databases.

In addition to following the FRE, HIM practitioners and providers must be familiar with their state's rules of evidence in conjunction with defining the content of the LHR. Many states have adopted the **Uniform Rules of Evidence** (modified in 2005).

Federal Rules of Civil Procedure

Federal rules are increasingly addressing the requirements for documents created and stored electronically to be admissible. These are the rules that provide much of the guidance related in this text related to e-discovery of electronic information. Figure 8.2 lists the cases that affect document production.

Additionally, notes appended to the FRE describe how the rules are being expanded to include electronic documentation. For example, FRE rule 901 (a) states:

> The requirement of authentication or identification as a condition precedent to admissibility is satisfied by evidence sufficient to support a finding that the matter in question is what its proponent claims.

Record Custodianship and Stewardship

The functions of a custodian of health records have been described as follows:

> An organization's record custodian defines the attributes of the LHR and manages its storage, access, release, and retention. The custodian presents the records into evidence when necessary, typically through the use of certified copies of documents. The custodian must attest that the records were kept in the normal course of daily business and

Figure 8.2. Cases that affect document production

- *Silvestri v. General Motors Corp* (271 F.3d 583, 591 (4th Cir 2001): The duty to preserve material evidence arises not only during litigation but also extends to that period before litigation when a party reasonably should know that the evidence may be relevant to anticipated litigation.

In addition to affecting document production, the following cases address sanctions for failure to preserve evidence.

- *QZO, Inc. v. Moyer,* 358 s.c. 246, 594 S.E. 2.d 541 (s.c. App. 2004)
- *Metropolitan Opera Ass'n v. Local 100* Hotel Employees and Restaurant Employees Intern. Union, 212 F.R.D. 178 (S.D.N.Y. 2003)
- *Leon v. IDX Sys Corp,* 464 F.3d. 951 ([A.qcwash.], 2006)
- *Plasse v. Tyco Electronics Corp.* 448 F. Supp. 2d 302 ([D.Mass.] 2006)

> that they are essentially accurate, trustworthy, and reliable. In order to attest to these factors the record custodian must have first-hand knowledge that these statements are true and accurate, therefore they must also manage the processes which help to document that the records do in fact meet these criteria (McLendon 2007 and 2010).

AHIMA also describes the health information custodian as the person designated responsible for the care, custody, and control of the health record for such persons or institutions that prepare and maintain records of healthcare. The official custodian or designee should be authorized to certify records and supervise all inspections and copying or duplication of records. The HIM professional or designee is often considered the custodian of the health record and may be called to testify to the admissibility of the record. He or she may be asked to verify the timeliness and normal business practices used to develop and maintain the health record.

Before EHRs became prevalent, a member of the HIM department typically served as the custodian of the organization's paper-based health records. This person was responsible for attesting to the authenticity of the records, especially when they are provided in response to a subpoena. With the movement to the EHR, the role of custodian may include other professionals within the organization.

Additionally, organizations should manage the record custodian function with clear internal policies to ensure that all who perform this role do so consistently and with an awareness that what they do, produce, and say can impact or reflect upon the organization. Such policies may define which subpoenas require discussion with legal counsel prior to answering, as well as staff training on how to handle subpoenas.

Data (or information) stewardship and information governance have increased in usage as record custodianship has expanded to include electronic records. The concept that record custodians is a limited role dealing with physical record maintenance is being replaced by a wider, more enterprise-wide view of information stewardship and governance is accurate, but it will take years or decades to be fully included into the law. Whatever name they are called by, the duties of those parties responsible for medical records are crucial to creation and maintenance of not only highly defensible records, but those that are used to meet ARRA requirements.

Enterprise content management (ECM) is a generic term describing software applications found in many non-healthcare business markets that has not really found a great deal of traction in healthcare. Usage of such systems is expected to increase over time due to their usefulness to manage the explosion of digital information being created and stored during the provision of care. These systems help organize and name the various data, information, documents, data, reports, files, videos, audio, and other file types into an easily indexed software-based structure. Custodians (stewards) will increasingly see these types of record management formalization tools being implemented and should plan on learning their operation as they are introduced.

Subpoenas and Orders for Production of Records

Subpoenas and orders to produce records are legal requests for patient information. Proper response to these requests relies on a provider having clearly defined the content of the LHR. Without such a definition, there may be inconsistency in the documentation released in response to a request from an attorney with patient authorization, or documentation released in response to a subpoena. Healthcare providers and facilities must clearly identify those documents, data elements, and so forth that are part of the LHR that will be maintained in accordance with state and federal laws.

Several types of subpoenas and orders to produce records are discussed below.

Subpoena Duces Tecum

Rule 17 of the FRCP provides that a subpoena is an order directing a person to appear and testify at a given time. A **subpoena duces tecum** requires the witness to bring certain documents with him or her when he or she testifies. Subpoenas can be issued by a court, grand jury, a lawyer representing a party in a civil or criminal lawsuit, or a government agency. A subpoena duces tecum can call for any number of things: Accounting documents, payroll records, corporate financial records, bank records, contracts, and computer records.

Some states allow for copies of the records to be mailed to the court when accompanied by the proper affidavits as to authenticity (for example, the State of California Consent Manual [CHA 2007]). When the subpoena duces tecum names the provider or healthcare entity as a defendant, the custodian of records must consult with legal counsel before responding. Once a representative of a healthcare facility receives a subpoena duces tecum, it is important that the organization cease any practice that results in the destruction or alteration of health information.

Subpoena Duces Tecum Re Deposition

Procedures for submitting a record in response to a subpoena duces tecum related to a deposition are the same as those for a subpoena duces tecum related to litigation. If a mailed response is allowed, the records will be sent to the requesting party. However, personal appearance often is required for a deposition.

Order for Production of Records and Court Orders

An order for production of records is a type of court order. A judge can compel a party in litigation to produce records even after that litigant has moved to quash (suppress or extinguish) a subpoena requesting the records. Failure to comply with an order for production of records can result in a litigant being placed in contempt.

Inspector General Subpoenas

The Office of the Inspector General (OIG) is empowered to require the attendance and testimony of witnesses and production of any other evidence at an investigational inquiry. An OIG subpoena can be issued in civil, criminal, or administrative proceedings (5 USC App. 3 § [6][a][4]). The same considerations discussed above with respect to a subpoena duces tecum apply to an OIG subpoena.

False Claims Act and HIPAA Administrative Subpoenas

The False Claims Act (31 USC § 3733) and HIPAA both provide for administrative subpoenas. These subpoenas can be enforced by the appropriate district court. An administrative subpoena under the False Claims Act is called a civil investigative demand (CID). A CID can compel the production of documents, require answers to interrogatories, and call for the provision of oral testimony. An administrative subpoena under HIPAA is called an authorized investigative demand. Under 18 USC § 3486, the attorney general or his or her designee can issue an investigative demand for any act or activity involving a federal healthcare offense.

Issues to Consider in Responding to Subpoenas and Orders for Production of Records

Some of the issues to consider in responding to subpoenas are detailed in this section.

Validating that the Format of the Request Meets State Legal Requirements

Generally, states require a particular form, with a seal or signature of an officer of the court (or attorney), addressed to the record custodian. HIPAA and some state laws require that the person who is the subject of the requested records be notified of the subpoena and provided an opportunity to quash the subpoena. HIM staff needs to be aware of the date requirements in their states and documentation related to the patient's notification or decision to attempt to quash any subpoena. The process for notifying the subject (patient) of subpoenaed records and the time period granted for a notification for the patient to quash the subpoena vary by state.

Determining if Healthcare Information May Be Disclosed

The attorneys involved in the legal proceeding will be concerned with the content of the request, privilege, and type of access to determine if healthcare information may be disclosed in the proceeding. Record custodians must carefully review any subpoena or order to produce records described in figure 8.3 and enlist the aid of their legal counsel any time they have questions or issues.

Content of Discovery Requests—Substance Abuse and Psychiatric Records

In most cases, a general subpoena does not cover substance abuse records or mental health records. Substance abuse records must be requested by court order. Depending on state law, mental health records may also need a court order or other special treatment.

Content of Discovery Requests—Pediatric Records

Records custodians should be familiar with their state's guidelines for release of information (ROI) for pediatric records. Many issues may affect pediatric records ROI guidelines, among them are identity of the custodial parent and incidents of child abuse.

Figure 8.3. Items for record custodian review

1. The subpoena meets state or federal requirements.
2. The subject of the records subpoenaed has been notified of the subpoena and given an opportunity to quash the order.
3. The subpoena names the correct institution and provider.
4. The subject of the records being subpoenaed was a patient of the provider. A certifying statement may be produced in response to the subpoena if the subject was never a patient.
5. The records being subpoenaed exist. If the records have been purged in accordance with retention laws, a certification of destruction may be produced.
6. The records being subpoenaed do not contain information related to diagnosis and treatment of substance abuse or mental illness.
7. The records being subpoenaed are those of a particular patient, not a general category of patients, for example, "all records of Dr. Smith from 1995 to 2005" or "all live birth records for the past year."

Content of Discovery Requests—Fishing Expeditions

In general, a party can move to have a subpoena set aside or quashed when the subpoena amounts to a "fishing expedition"—that is, the party seeking the documents is trying to find out whether a responding party has any documents that would assist the requesting party's case. The fact that electronic record systems may produce a wide variety of data does not change the response to this type of subpoena. HIM practitioners and providers should consult with legal counsel if they suspect that a subpoena is a fishing expedition.

Privilege

Hospital records and other health records are generally within the scope of the physician-patient privilege. A hospital may assert the privilege on behalf of its patients. However, the privilege cannot be raised when the patient or the patient's survivors or estate seek access to the patient's own health records over the hospital's objection or if the case involves criminal proceedings and the records are evidence in the proceeding. Similarly, subjects of worker's compensation arbitration subpoenas cannot assert privilege.

Legal (Litigation) Hold and Suspension of Document Destruction

The new federal rules (and perhaps others) allow for a legal (litigation) hold to be placed on documents, including electronic documents. This hold prohibits the documents from being purged or otherwise destroyed, even in accordance with a pre-established destruction and purging process. Custodians of health records must be made aware of any such holds to suspend a purge and destruction process. In addition, the custodian of records must communicate such a hold to the IT director or system administrator for any system that contains patient information that is designated a part of the LHR, so that no individual system inadvertently purges or otherwise destroys information under a litigation hold.

Document Production—Paper or Electronic

Responding to a subpoena follows the same process whether the records are maintained in paper or electronic format. Most often, electronic records will need to be printed and added to any files maintained in paper format.

Admissibility of Health Records

In order to be admissible, health records must meet the definition of business records and other requirements established by the FRE and state rules. With the addition of electronically generated or stored records, the validity and integrity of the records may become an issue. Thus, record custodians may be required to provide substantiating information about the system(s) that are used to produce or store patient information. This is done to satisfy concerns that the systems allow only authorized users to enter or correct patient information, clearly identify the author, provide date and time of data entries, and prevent corruption of data or unauthorized access that could invalidate the information (AHIMA 2005).

Methods and Circumstances of Preparation

Typically, state regulations address the methodologies to be used in preparing records or record copies for submission to courts under the discovery process (for example, the State of California Consent Manual [CHA 2007]). Federal requirements also exist, which have recently been updated by the new electronic discovery rule documented in the FRCP. Details of these new processes are described in two articles from the *Journal of American Health Information Management Association:* "Developing a Litigation Response Plan" (Baldwin-Stried 2007), and "The New Electronic Discovery Civil Rule" (AHIMA e-HIM Work Group on e-Discovery 2006).

Typically, records requested in response to a federal subpoena or court order must be certified as business records and submitted directly to the clerk of the court or a judge.

If an in-person response is requested, the record custodian must be prepared to swear to the authenticity of the records and answer questions about the circumstances under which they were created, processed, and stored.

Chapter 9

Other Key EHR Concepts

The information, both patient identifiable and related metadata, contained within an EHR application may take several forms. The formats include those listed in figure 9.1, Metadata Formats.

A key question to ask when considering your LHR definition is: What format of EHR output do the courts require for the designated business records to be admitted into evidence? The following points will help you address this question:

- Courts that need to view and receive certified copies of medical records today overwhelmingly use the term "*documents*." Therefore, any EHR must *efficiently* address documents. Paper or document formats in either Microsoft Word, PDF, or scanned image formats are typically submitted. Many courts are moving toward electronic filing, but even so, they work with formalized documents, not simply a view of data from an EHR database.
- After recognizing the courts' reliance on documents, it is logical to infer that documents and data output are required from an EHR and must be produced efficiently. This argues that HIM processes must be managed effectively by EHR platforms. Various EHR systems have varying degrees of efficiency in managing paper output and record management operations. These attributes should be considered any time EHR systems are strategized, designed, procured, and implemented, and they must be evaluated during your LHR definition processes.

Print and various other forms of output are clearly here to stay. There has been a bit of misunderstanding about the continued role of paper and other various forms of EHR output. In fact, many parties assume printing *just goes away* with automation. However, it is becoming clear that in addition to serving the needs of the provider of care, the EHR must provide well-developed output functionalities. Output is here to stay, and structured clinical data will eventually enjoy widespread adoption. Therefore, output

Figure 9.1. Metadata formats

- **Documents** (word processing files and transcriptions) that have properties allowing their manipulation in common native formats such as rich text format (RTF), extensible markup language (XML), or Microsoft Word (such as update, edit, delete, redact, amend) and stable, permanent storage.
- **Messages** can be between system users, or patients and providers, data exchanges, personal health records, ambulatory, and inpatient providers. These functionalities relate to written intra-health team and external communications. Sometimes the term *secure messaging* may be more descriptive. The questions to be answered include if and how are they encrypted, if they allow attachments, administrator, and how privacy is protected and presented within legal proceedings. Are secure (or unsecure) messages defined by the record custodian as part of your legal record for disclosure? They probably should not be, it's a facility decision, but knowing which messages contain relevant PHI about an individual patient, especially if multiple patients were discussed within one message, is very hard to detect and manage. Messages may not be reasonably accessible for initial record disclosure subpoenas but it is a popular trend for messages to be requested as part of e-discovery. Messaging also includes messages that are used during clinician alerts and reminders.
- **Metadata** are data that describe, index, and otherwise relate to patient-identifiable information or system operational data contained within an EHR (for example, audit logs).
- **Output** is what a user sees on an EHR screen and is a representation of data (structured and unstructured) contained within a database that can be manipulated within the EHR application itself. Output cannot "live" outside the EHR application code, so these are not considered documents per se. Rather, documents may consist of reports driven from structured data within an EHR, as well as other electronic documents that can be managed in a common native document format, such as Microsoft Word, XML, or portable document format (PDF). These document types may be created by report writer software and may be portable outside the EHR application. Regardless of which electronic format is used, documents absolutely require output via printing or otherwise into physical form (typically paper). This is not always easily accomplished as a user functionality from all vendor applications and must be evaluated during your LHR definition process. Electronic documents within an EHR can be exported outside the system as either print outputs to paper, as faxes, e-mails, or interfaced messages. Lately there has been a call for image export onto CDs or DVDs instead of paper copies, although this is not currently routine for submission into evidence. Many EHR systems lack the capability to produce copies of documents onto discs. Even many document management systems cannot perform this function, but this will change as Meaningful Use requirements become mandatory.
- **Structured, discrete data within a database** include such items such as lab values for sodium that can be plotted and graphed as well as reported in numeric values. These are the most valuable data that can be mined through the use of report writer software.
- **Unstructured data** are information such as transcribed documents where a provider of care dictates in stream of consciousness. This data can also be mined via technologies such as natural language processing (NLP), but with less specificity and more set up overhead than discrete data elements.

functionality needs to be accommodated efficiently by all EHR platforms. Unfortunately, to date, these functionalities have been found to be poorly created and crude in operation within many EHR platforms as their designers mistakenly attached low significance to these functions. The HL7 Legal Health Record Functional Profile should elevate the importance of these functionalities going forward. Additional regulations and standards are discussed below.

Medicare Conditions of Participation

Medicare regulations contain detailed Conditions of Participation for Hospitals, some of which affect a hospital's obligations with respect to the creation and maintenance of health records, thereby informing the definition of the LHR (42 CFR Part 482). Medicare regulations also contain Conditions of Participation requirements for long-term care facilities (42 CFR Part 483), home health agencies (42 CFR Part 484), specialized providers (42 CFR Part 485), and laboratories (42 CFR Part 493). Part 482 of the Conditions of Participation for Hospitals, Subpart C, Section 482.24(c), detailing the general standards for health record content are included in figure 9.2.

To participate in the Medicare program, providers are required to abide by all Conditions of Participation, including those related to creating and maintaining health records. HIM professionals at the facility level should be intimately familiar with the Conditions of Participation that pertain to their settings.

Check for specialized patient types as well as documentation requirements, and specific citations from both the Joint Commission and the Conditions of Participation for Hospitals.

Medicare Billing Guidance

The Centers for Medicare and Medicaid Services (CMS) publishes a series of manuals to provide guidance to Medicare providers with respect to compliance and billing practices. Several sections in these manuals describe the documentation required to prove that a service was, in fact, provided, or that it was medically necessary and, thereby, suitable for reimbursement. For example, the Hospital Manual (DHHS 2006) provides:

> 210.8 Physical Therapy Furnished by the Hospital or by Others under Arrangements with the Hospital and under Its Supervision.
>
> A. General. To be covered, physical therapy services must relate directly and specifically to an active *written treatment regimen* established by the physician after any needed consultation with the qualified physical therapist and must be reasonable and necessary to the treatment of the individual's illness or injury.

Figure 9.2. General standards for health record content

The medical record must contain information to justify admission and continued hospitalization, support the diagnosis, and describe the patient's progress and response to medications and services.

1. All entries must be legible and complete, and must be authenticated and dated promptly by the person (identified by name and discipline) who is responsible for ordering, providing, or evaluating the service furnished.
   a. The author of each entry must be identified and must authenticate his or her entry.
   b. Authentication may include signatures, written initials, or computer entry.
2. All records must document the following, as appropriate:
   a. Evidence of a physical examination, including a health history, performed no more than 7 days prior to admission or within 48 hours after admission.
   b. Admitting diagnosis
   c. Results of all consultative evaluations of the patient and appropriate findings by clinical and other staff involved in the care of the patient
   d. Documentation of complications, hospital acquired infections, and unfavorable reactions to drugs and anesthesia
   e. Properly executed informed consent forms for procedures and treatments specified by the medical staff, or by Federal or State law if applicable, to require written patient consent
   f. All practitioners' orders, nursing notes, reports of treatment, medication records, radiology, and laboratory reports, and vital signs and other information necessary to monitor the patient's condition.
   g. Discharge summary with outcome of hospitalization, disposition of case, and provisions for follow-up care.
   h. Final diagnosis with completion of health records within 30 days following discharge.

Other parts provide additional health record requirements, for example:

482.23—Nursing Services
482.26—Radiologic Services
482.27—Laboratory Services
482.51—Surgical Services
482.52—Anesthesia Services
482.53—Nuclear Medicine Services
482.61 and 424.14—Psychiatric Hospitals
482.66—Swing Beds
483.75—Long Term Care Facilities
484.48 and 424.22—Home Health Agencies
485.60 and 424.27—Comprehensive Outpatient Rehab Facilities

Source: Part 482 of the Conditions of Participation for Hospitals, Subpart C, Section 482.24(c).

State Regulations for Health Record Content

Most of the requirements of the Conditions of Participation for Hospitals are included in the department of health licensing regulations for various states. However, details can vary, so a provider must check individual state laws for the specific regulations related to health record content. The variation in state requirements requires careful research because specific requirements may be located in different sections of the regulations.

HIPAA Designated Record Set

The Health Information Portability and Accountability Act (HIPAA) is a federal law aimed at protecting patient privacy and facilitating patients' access to their own health records as needed. Accordingly, providers must consider HIPAA and the regulations promulgated in developing a definition of the legal heath record at their organizations.

This act resulted in standards that define processes and practices for healthcare providers, payers, and clearinghouses to follow in protecting the confidentiality and security of patient information. Section 164.501 of the Privacy Standards requires providers to define a designated record set (figure 9.3).

Because of this standard, a provider may already have enumerated various documents and data elements as belonging to the designated record set. This designated record set may be reviewed to determine which of the various documents or data elements listed should be included as documents and data elements that comprise the content of the LHR.

The LHR intersects with the DRS in that the LHR should be offered for views, copies, amendments, and similar HIPAA patient rights. This will not always be possible. Sometimes a greater set of information than the formally defined LHR will need to be addressed within the HIPAA request, as the DRS is larger than the LHR in scope. But record managers are wise to utilize the LHR as often as possible to fulfill HIPAA-based requests.

However, depending on context of request, not all of the information or documents contained in a designated record set will be part of the LHR. For example, the documents or data may not meet the requirements of the FRE and thus will not be included in response to a federal court order. Specifically, the health records from other providers or e-mails may not meet the FRE as it may be difficult to verify the author of an e-mail or certify the validity of documents sent from other providers, as is required by the business record exception to the hearsay rule contained in the FRE. Such documents, however, may be required to be maintained as part of the designated record set.

Figure 9.3. Sample of a designated record set

A designated record set (DRS) is a group of records maintained by or for a covered entity (healthcare provider, payer, or clearinghouse) that includes:

- The health and billing records about individuals maintained by or for a covered healthcare provider
- The enrollment, payment, claims adjudication, and case or medical management record systems maintained by or for a health plan
- *Information used in whole or in part by or for the covered entity to make decisions about individuals* (Hughes 2003 64A)—this is a key component of the definition as it expands the scope of the DRS to include any information used to make a decision about an individual (patient). This means even scraps of paper and Post-it™ notes can be a part of the designated record set that individuals have the right to view, copy, request amendments, etc. Literally all of the patient identifiable information within a healthcare facility and a great deal of operational data as well is considered a part of the Designated Record Set.

This definition includes all of the following:

- Contents of a paper-based health record
- Information included in a computer-based record environment
- Content of the patient account file or patient account database
- Copies of records from other providers used to make decisions about the individual:
  - o Such as hospital records for a long-term care facility referral
  - o E-mail communications
  - o Research databases

Source: AHIMA Practice Brief: Defining the Designated Record Set (DRS)

By reviewing the documents and data elements contained in the designated record set, a HIM practitioner or healthcare provider begins to focus the scope of information to be included in the content of the LHR.

Requests for information also must meet minimum mandatory restrictions calling for exclusion of all record components that are not related to the request. This concept does not apply as well for legal requests, that is, subpoenas. There must be a balance maintained between what is required for disclosure subsequent to a request for records, be it via subpoena, court order, or similar, as in general the record custodian is required to provide what is listed on the request and providing too much information, which may violate minimum necessary principals. This is why all complex legal requests should be reviewed with your legal counsel, under legal privilege, if possible.

Accrediting Body Requirements

Most healthcare facilities participate in some type of accreditation process. The organizations conducting the accreditation surveys publish standards that must be met in order for a facility to receive accreditation status. These standards include requirements for health record documentation.

In order to receive Joint Commission accreditation, acute care hospitals, long-term care facilities, home health agencies, hospices, substance abuse facilities, behavioral health providers, and managed care organizations must comply with standards issued by the commission. Various other accreditation bodies and standards can be found within the healthcare marketplace. Whichever accreditation is utilized, providers who seek accreditation from one or more organizations need to consider the standards of the accrediting body in the definition of their LHR.

Accreditation standards also exist for other aspects of healthcare. For example, two accrediting bodies exist for medical education—Association of American Medical Colleges (AAMC) and Liaison Committee on Medical Education (LCME). HIM professionals should familiarize themselves with the accreditations recommended not only for their facilities but also for the physicians, allied health professionals, and other staff members.

Payer Requirements

Various payers may have requirements for the types of documentation they require to substantiate a claim or request for services. As representatives from payer organizations often review health records, the LHR should include these types of documentation.

Requirements vary from state to state; therefore it is recommended that HIM professionals and health law attorneys familiarize themselves with the requirements for their state. AHIMA members may find information through their Component State Associations (CSAs).

Other Standards

Some of the additional EHR standards that have been developed are detailed in this section. These include the HL7 Functional Model, ASTM Standard Practice for Content and Structure, and core data sets.

HL7 Functional Model

Health Level Seven (HL7) is an American National Standards Institute (ANSI) standards organization that originated the de facto standard for moving patient information between healthcare applications. In 2004, the HL7 group developed an EHR system draft standard for trial use (EHR-S DSTU). These standards focus more on the technical functionality of an EHR system than on the content of the EHR.

The EHR-S functional model paves the way for a legal EHR. According to Michelle Dougherty, RHIA, CHP, director of practice leadership at AHIMA, who is jointly leading the development of the legal EHR profile (HL7 2007):

> It is important that the EHR stand as a legal record for business purpose, otherwise it forces the paper record to serve as the LHR—causing providers' administrative burden and the additional cost of keeping both paper and electronic records. The EHR-S contains listed functionalities that help providers maintain a legal EHR for business, regulatory, and accreditation purposes.

The slowly growing set of standards from HL7 that directly affect record managers and EHR system developers is not yet widely adopted by EHR system developers, but over time will serve as an important source of functionalities that all EHRs should provide. The HL7 Record Management and Evidentiary Standards (RM & ES) serve as baselines for much of the functionality within EHRs that manage the aspects crucial to LHR functionalities listed previously in this text.

The AHIMA Practice Brief: Understanding the EHR-S Functional Model, provides a detailed overview of these functional standards. However, according to the practice brief, there are two HL7 EHR work groups charged with evaluating the functionality in the draft standard to ensure that it can stand as a legal record (Dougherty 2005, 64D). Providers should continue to monitor the HL7 Web site (http://www.HL7.org) to obtain the latest recommendations from these work groups. The latest functional model can be found online from HL7 (http://www.hl7.org/EHR/).

ASTM Standard Practice for Content and Structure

American Society for Testing and Materials (ASTM) subcommittee 31.28 has published the Standard Practice for Content and Structure of the EHR. See figure 9.4.

Core Data Sets

Core data sets are defined as "the shareable electronic patient demographic and essential 'persistent' clinical information necessary to provide informed medical care"

(AHIMA Workgroup 2004). Core data sets provide a format and/or a structure for entities to transfer patient information from one entity to another. Many organizations have defined a core data set of patient information. There are no standards for such sets and no agreement on a standard data set to be used for all purposes.

The AHIMA Practice Brief: E-HIM Strategic Initiative: Core Data Sets, which suggests core data set content, does not carry the weight of regulatory authority, but it does provide data elements to be considered in establishing an LHR (AHIMA Workgroup 2004).

The AHIMA e-HIM Work Group on Core Data for the Physician Practice EHR developed eight clinical workflow core data sets for use in physician offices. See figure 9.5.

Figure 9.4. ASTM Standard Practice for Content and Structure of the EHR

1. Identify the content and logical structure of an EHR consistent with currently acknowledged patient record content. The record carries all health-related information about a person over time. It may include history and physical, laboratory tests, diagnostic reports, orders and treatments documentation, patient identifying information, legal permissions, and so on.
2. Explain the relationship of data coming from diverse sources (for example, clinical laboratory information management systems, order entry systems, pharmacy information management systems, and dictation systems) and other data in the EHR as the primary repository for information from various sources.
3. Provide a common vocabulary for those developing, purchasing, and implementing an EHR.
4. Provide sufficient content from which data extracts can be compiled to create unique setting views.

Figure 9.5. Clinical workflow core data sets for use in physician offices

1. Pediatric well patient clinical workflow: New patient
2. Pediatric well patient clinical workflow: Established patient
3. Pediatric sick patient clinical workflow: New patient
4. Pediatric sick patient clinical workflow: Established patient
5. Adult well patient clinical workflow: New patient
6. Adult well patient clinical workflow: Established patient
7. Adult sick patient clinical workflow: New patient
8. Adult sick patient clinical workflow: Established patient

Source: AHIMA e-HIM Work Group on Core Data for the Physician Practice EHR

These data sets are fully documented in AHIMA Practice Brief: Core Data Sets for the Physician Practice EHR (AHIMA e-HIM Work Group 2003). These data sets identify the recommended documentation for a clinical encounter and should be considered in establishing the definition of the LHR for a physician's office.

One of the most widely publicized core data sets is the Continuity of Care Record (CCR). Developed by ASTM, the Massachusetts Medical Society, the Healthcare Information and Management Systems Society, the American Academy of Family Physicians, and the American Academy of Pediatrics, this data set is used by healthcare providers (primarily in Massachusetts) to transmit key data elements from one healthcare setting to another. CCD and a similar HL7 CCR (Continuity of Care Record) developed by HL7 are summary documents drawn from EHR data, sometimes automatically and are utilized within the ARRA Meaningful Use criteria. Since these documents are often created by the system and not authenticated by a provider of care, their use in legal proceedings is yet to be determined, unless they are directly tied to care delivery.

Metadata

Metadata are the "data about data" that facilitate the understanding, use, and management of digital information. See figure 9.6 for samples of metadata. Metadata can be fully discoverable in civil litigation.

The term ***legal discovery*** refers to the act or process of finding or learning something previously not known, with the purpose or intent of using it as evidence in a criminal or civil legal case. Today, with the prevalence of electronically stored data and the ease of searching digital data, the discovery process is focusing less on paper-based searches and more on computer-based searches, or e-discovery. More information about e-discovery can be found at http://SearchSecurity.com. Failure to comply with e-discovery orders can lead to the negative consequences listed in figure 9.7.

Figure 9.6. Samples of metadata

- Identification information (such as: file/author name, company name, name/number of computer used to create the document, date created/modified/accessed/printed, and file/network path location)
- Document version numbers
- Revision history
- Data inserted by a document management system (for example, client/customer ID number and document categorization information)

Figure 9.7. Negative consequences of failure to comply with e-discovery orders

Monetary penalties. For examples, see:

- *Procter & Gamble vs Haugen,* 179 F.R.D. 622 (D. Utah, 1998).
- *In re Prudential Insurance Company of America Sales Practice Litigation,* 169 F.R.D. 598 (D.N.J.1997).

Loss of the ability to call witnesses. For example, see:

- *United States v. Philip Morris USA, Inc,* 327 F. Supp 2d 21 (D.D.C. 2004).

Adverse instructions to the jury. For example, see:

- *Zubulake v. UBS Warburg LLC,* 229 F.R.D. 422 (S.D.N.Y. 2004)

Default judgment. For example, see:

- *Essex Group v. Express Wire Services Inc.,* 157 N.C. App. 306, 578.5 S.E. 2d 705 (N.C. App. 2003)

Additionally, organizations that routinely scrub (remove metadata from) their systems and files can risk fines and other legal sanctions. Therefore, when an organization defines the content of its LHRs, it should consider including metadata fields along with patient information. Such metadata would include, for example, creation date, date sent, date received, last access date, and last modification data.

HIM professionals and health law attorneys should research their states' case law to determine:

- Who will impose the fines and other legal sanctions
- Whether or not metadata are discoverable
- The existence of records retention regulations

Impact of EHRs on Legal Processes

Advances in information technology are increasing the amount of information collected and made available about an individual. A patient's health record may now contain information from multiple facilities and healthcare providers. As a result, those responsible for managing patient information must define the subset of information that will be used as the LHR. The LHR must be maintained in a secure manner that does not call into question its validity or authenticity.

During the transition of the health record from paper to electronic medium, record custodians must ensure that all pertinent documentation is stored for as long as required by record retention guidelines set by the provider organization, but many times following guidelines for their facility from state, federal, corporate, and other sources.

Scope of Information to Be Released

The EHR expands the scope of patient information beyond that traditionally included in the paper record. In addition to the standard components of paper health records, the EHR may now contain such detailed information as the results of diagnostic tests—films, videos, tracings, and so forth. The new scope of information made possible by the EHR impacts the definition of the LHR, as well as its validity as a legal document, and the processes healthcare organizations must follow in responding to subpoenas and other legitimate requests for release of records.

Regardless of the medium of health record documentation, the information still belongs to the patient, and the laws related to the need for a patient authorization to release information still apply. The record custodian may now be responsible for more health records and patient information databases, due to the expanding scope and complexity of healthcare organizations. The record custodian, for example, may be involved with ROI and processing subpoenas for records from multiple facilities, clinics, treatment centers, and physician's offices. This expanded responsibility is the result of two phenomena:

1. Various business arrangements among healthcare providers, such as integrated delivery networks, multispecialty group practices, and so forth
2. The growth of centralized data repositories, integrated health information exchange networks, and other arrangements that encompass information from multiple sources

As a result, the record custodian may be required to deal with multiple LHR definitions, each of which represents a different provider and record set.

Patient authorizations as well as subpoenas or other orders for record production need to be scrutinized to determine which records are to be included. An authorization or order to produce records for a particular hospital might not cover production of all of the records from other institutions, providers, or business associates linked with the specific hospital named. If the authorization or order is only valid for the LHR defined by the hospital, care must be taken to release only those documents and data specified in and covered by the authorization or order.

Reassessing Access and Disclosure Policies and Procedures

A request for information from an attorney may be subsequently followed by a subpoena. Some attorneys use this technique to impugn the validity of a record because the requested record and the subpoenaed record differ—especially if there is a gap of several weeks or months between the two requests. One reason to define the content of the LHR is to avoid having two different versions of documents submitted in response to two different requests for the same information.

Disclosure of Information to the Designated Recipient

States generally prescribe the manner in which records may be presented to the court—whether by mail or in person. All generally require a certificate of authenticity of the record, typically an affidavit from the record custodian. Records requested by a judge via court order must be directed specifically to the judge, rather than to the court clerk. With an EHR, an additional certificate of authentication may also need to be submitted by a software developer.

Maintaining Your LHR

All healthcare providers must establish P & Ps to maintain the health record in a way that establishes its validity, preserves its integrity, and facilitates efficient and timely response to legally permissible requests. Some record management considerations to factor into your LHR policies and procedures are listed below.

Accuracy

Accurate documentation in a health record should reflect the true, correct, and exact description of the care delivered for both content and timing. The accuracy and the completeness of the entries in the health record are the responsibility of the author(s) and are governed by the organization's P & Ps, which should include documentation standards based on the regulations, standards, and other sources noted in chapter 2. Any decision regarding the inclusion or exclusion of information in the content of the LHR should be noted in the P & P documentation.

Addenda, Amendments, Corrections, and Other Documentation Issues

Providers must have a process in place for handling addenda, amendments, corrections, and deletions in health record documentation. When healthcare providers determine that patient care documentation is inaccurate or incomplete, they must follow the established P & Ps to ensure the integrity of the record.

The American Society for Testing and Materials (ASTM) and HL7 have established recommended technical requirements and standards for EHR systems. (See chapter 2.)

Organizational policy should delineate the timeframes within which the corrections and deletions can be made and outline what is necessary to make amendments to the record. The corrected or deleted information should be apparent in the original system, as well as in any other systems that received the original information. The system needs to maintain a record or audit trail of the correction or deletion, including the date of change, the incorrect value or text, and the identity (ID) of the individual making the correction or deletion. While the original data or document may be hidden from view, it must be retained and made available for viewing when necessary.

An ***addendum*** is an entry used to provide additional information in conjunction with a previous entry. With this type of correction, a previous note has been made, and the addendum provides additional information to address a specific situation or incident. An *amendment* is a separate entry used to correct information in a previous entry.

For text reports, changes should be made by creating an addendum to the original report. Here, the **original document**'s identifying information should be noted in the addendum, along with the date of correction, and the identity and authorization of the individual completing the addendum. See figure 9.8.

Authorship

An **author** is a person or system who originates or creates information that becomes part of the record. Each author must be granted permission by the healthcare entity to make such entries and not all users will be granted authorship rights into all areas of the EHR. The individual must have the credentials required by state and federal laws to be granted the right to document observations and facts related to the providing of healthcare services. Through the medical staff bylaws or rules and regulations, and through documentation guidelines, a provider will indicate the type and frequency of entries to be made in the health record. Often, the bylaws, rules and regulations, or

Figure 9.8. Actions to perform when making an addendum

- Document the current date and time
- Write "addendum" and state the reason for the addendum, referring back to the original entry
- Identify any sources of information used to support the addendum
- Complete the addendum as soon after the original note as possible
- In an electronic system, provide a link to the original entry or insert a symbol by the original entry to indicate the existence of the addendum

guidelines are based on the documentation requirements published by various government and regulatory agencies. (See chapter 2.)

Corrections

Proper procedures must be followed when correcting documentation problems or mistakes. ASTM and HL7 have issued standards that apply to error correction. The principles followed in making corrections to paper documents can also be followed when making corrections to electronic documentation. See figure 9.9.

The system must have the ability to track corrections or changes to the entry once the entry has been entered or authenticated. An individual viewing the record should see an indicator that a new or additional entry has resulted and should also be able to see the new information. It must be clear to the user that there are additional versions of the data being viewed. Additional information related to error corrections can be found in AHIMA Practice Brief: Maintaining a Legally Sound Health Record—Paper and Electronic (2005).

Cut, Paste, and Copy Forward

While the technology used to support the EHR can provide many enhancements over the paper record (for example, multiple simultaneous access and audit trails), it can also present the potential for weakening the integrity of the information. One such risk occurs with the cut, copy, and paste functionality present in many operating system and software programs. This functionality allows a user to highlight all or a portion of a document or screen display, cut (delete) the text, or copy and then paste the portion into a different or new document, potentially overwriting the original text.

For individuals who write letters, papers, articles, and so forth, this functionality is very useful. However, when a physician instructs a transcriptionist to copy the body

Figure 9.9. Actions to perform when correcting an entry in a computerized health record system

- View the original entry
- Enter the current date and time
- Identify the person making the change
- Note the reason for the change
- Verify that a hard copy printed from the EHR reflects the correction

of a history and physical exam from one patient into the report of another patient, the functionality becomes potentially dangerous. Risks from the improper use of the cut, copy, and paste function include those listed in figure 9.10.

Providers need to create P & Ps around the use of the cut, copy, and paste function. Providers may decide to prohibit the use of the functionality. When providers decide that the functionality may be used, they need to set criteria for and establish restrictions on use of the functionality. For example, the provider may stipulate that only the original author can copy information from one document to another, or that text from the record of one patient cannot be cut and pasted into the record of another patient. See AHIMA Practice Brief: Maintaining a Legally Sound Health Record—Paper and Electronic (2005); and AHIMA's Guidelines for EHR documentation to prevent fraud (2007) and its accompanying Appendix B: Case Studies.

Late Entries

Late entries occur when a pertinent entry is missed or is not written in a timely manner. When a late entry is documented, it should be clearly identified as a late entry. The author of the entry needs to record the current date and time, as well as the date of the event that is the subject of the late entry. The author should also refer to counsel or any sources of information or circumstances surrounding the late entry. The longer the time period between the occurrence of the event and the recording of the late entry, the less reliable the information entered becomes.

Patient-requested Amendments

Healthcare organizations need policies to address how patients and their representatives can request amendments to their health records. 45 CFR 164.526(a) of the HIPAA standards requires specific procedures and timeframes be followed for processing a patient's request for an amendment. A separate entry—such as a progress

Figure 9.10. Some risks from the improper use of the cut, paste, and copy forward function

- Cutting, rather than copying text from the original document and, thus, deleting important information from the patient's record
- Pasting incorrect information into the document of the other patient, which could affect treatment
- Pasting the information into the wrong patient's record
- Creating the implication that a record was tampered with

note, form, or typed letter—can be used for patient amendment documentation. The amendment should:

- Refer back to the information questioned, by type of document or information, and the date and time of the original entry
- Document the information believed to be inaccurate and the information the patient or legal representative believes to be correct

The documentation in question must not be removed from the health record or obliterated in any way. The patient cannot require that the documentation be removed or deleted.

Templates, Boilerplates, Canned Text, and Structured Input

Care must be taken that devices such as templates, boilerplates, canned text, and structured input support clinical care and accurate documentation, and are not used simply to expedite the documentation process. Creation and periodic review of these tools should be based on clinically appropriate, standards-based protocols for common or routine information. Documentation by these methods should require an active choice by the provider of care. When a clinician reviews and authenticates an entry in a patient's health record, the author is indicating that he or she reviewed and completed the documentation and accepts its accuracy as his or her own.

Chapter 10

Conclusion

Learning Points

- Recognize that defining the LHR is an ongoing and evolving process
- Understand the true breadth of LHR content

There are certain factors that work with EHR system attributes and their supporting processes to validate document, data, and report accuracy, trustworthiness, and reliability. Performing ongoing maintenance of your LHR is certainly one of these factors. Ongoing maintenance of your LHR includes understanding and ensuring that your EHR system's functionalities continue to meet standards that help meet the highest degree of LHR protections and data integrity. The LHR knowledge base is rapidly expanding and, like all EHR processes, continually evolving, as is the record custodian's role. One of the primary challenges is to keep up with this evolution.

It is worth considering keeping the team or committee that is managing your LHR processes intact even after the bulk of the front-end definitions, policies, and procedures are completed. At least quarterly, review and update the current LHR policies and environment to help ensure up-to-date LHR process and validity.

The LHR is a subset of EHR documents, data, and content. Your organization must formally define and establish P & Ps detailing the components that define your LHR. Continue to define and build your LHR with an eye toward output and the elements of the systems that buttress the acceptance of documents, data, and content based upon accepted legal standards of accuracy, trustworthiness, and reliability. Remember that e-mail, aggregate data, health information exchange data, and metadata from many sources may be encompassed in any and all requests. Therefore, the scope of your LHR preparation and definition must be as wide as possible to ensure the highest levels of protection for your organization and litigation response procedures should be planned well in advance of their being needed for litigation.

Appendix A

Glossary

Definitions of terms are absolutely crucial to all legal processes. For example, well-written contracts always contain definitions of the included elements. Electronic records in healthcare have, in the recent past, generally suffered from a lack of timely, clear, concise, and standards-based definitions and naming conventions (or taxonomy) at the very highest levels. This lack of definition and nomenclature creates confusion among not only the users of the records, but also the functional developers and architects of both the strategies surrounding LHRs and the application platforms that put the concepts into practice. HL7 and other standards (see appendix B), along with use based on governmental statute and regulation terminology have stabilized some of the common phraseology referring to electronic health records, but is still lacking in others. An example of a term lacking significant standardized use is hybrid records, which seems to have an almost unlimited number of specific definitions dependent upon record systems operational at healthcare provider sites. This is compounded by the high number of software applications (referred to as EHR Modules in ARRA) that form a "complete EHR."

The following definitions are commonly utilized in healthcare record management practice. They may or may not be based in standards or even the *only* typically used definition. Rather, the terms listed below are a combination of the most common parlance in the industry and what the author of this text believes to be a clear statement of the ideas to be conveyed. This list illustrates the problem with a less-than-optimal set of standards-based definitions in any industry—a lack of clarity for all users of the terms that creates confusion among everyone striving to communicate and understand a complex field such as health record management.

Accounting of disclosure: HIPAA requirement to list, upon patient request, all disclosures that meet the criteria. In the past, this did not require accounting for disclosures for Treatment, Payment, and Operations (TPO), but under ARRA this changed to include these disclosures.

Addendum: An entry used to provide additional information in conjunction with a previous entry.

American Recovery and Reinvestment (ARRA) Act of 2009: A law that aims to "create new jobs and save existing ones, spur economic activity and invest in long-term growth, and foster unprecedented levels of accountability and transparency in government spending." Also known as the Stimulus Plan. http://www.recovery.gov/About/Pages/The_Act.aspx.

Any and all records: A phrase frequently used by attorneys in the discovery phase of a legal proceeding. Subpoena-based requests containing this phrase may create a situation where the record custodian or provider's legal counsel can work to limit the records disclosed to those defined by a particular healthcare entity's **legal health record**. Typically, this is only during a subpoena phase, unless the information is legally privileged or similarly protected, the discovery phase of litigation probably can be used to request any and all relevant materials.

Author: Person or system that originates or creates information that becomes part of the record.

Business record: (1) A record made or received in conjunction with a business purpose and preserved as evidence or because the information has potential value. (2) Information that is created, received, and maintained as evidence. (3) Information created by an organization or person—pursuant to legal obligation or in the transaction of business—that consistently delivers a full and accurate record.

Core data sets: "The shareable electronic patient demographic and essential 'persistent' clinical information necessary to provide informed medical care" (AHIMA Workgroup 2004).

Custodian: *See* Record custodian.

Data: (1) Basic facts about people, processes, measurements, and conditions represented by dates, numerical statistics, images, and symbols. (2) An unprocessed collection of raw facts, concepts, or instructions in a manner suitable for communication, interpretation, or processing by humans or automatic means.

Data element: A combination of one or more data entities that forms a unit or piece of information, such as patient identifier, a diagnosis, or treatment.

Disclosure: (1) The act of releasing, upon proper authorization, copies of business or medical records. (2) The output and release upon request of appropriate medical record documents. (3) The processes for releasing information to external sources' EHR data.

e-Discovery: (1) The discovery of electronic patient records that may be used for litigation or further legal proceedings. (2) e-Discovery is the process of legal discovery that takes place within electronic or electronic and paper hybrid records during the various phases of litigation. (Although e-discovery reflects an emphasis on electronic records, paper and hybrid records may also be included.)

Electronic document management systems (EDMS): Also referred to as Document Management or Imaging systems. These computer systems scan documents and capture electronically-interfaced documents to create repositories of information that also may have Business Process Management (BPM) type workflow and application programs, such as chart completion and electronic signatures. Many times EDMS systems are used to help define a legal health record for disclosure.

Electronic health record (EHR): Fully interconnected healthcare records in which previous test results, medications, and treatments are available for each new provider to ensure continuity of care.

Electronic medical record (EMR): A non-standardized term for the EHR. Typically refers to ambulatory provider electronic medical records.

Evidence: (1) Information that a fact finder may use to decide an issue. (2) Information that makes a fact or issue before court or other hearing more or less probable.

Federal Rules of Civil Procedure (FRCP): Rules established by the U.S. Supreme Court setting the 'rules of the road' and procedures for federal court cases. FRCP were amended in 2006 to include electronic records and continue to be very important as benchmarks in how these records can be used in courts, not only federal, but state and other courts as well. Record custodianship is widely discussed within the FRCP.

Federal Rules of Evidence (FRE): Rules established by the U.S. Supreme Court guiding the introduction and sue of evidence in federal court proceedings that are an important benchmark for state and other courts. Federal Rules of Evidence will govern what and how electronic records may be used, and the roles of record custodianship.

Health information exchanges (HIEs): Data exchanges and their facilitating infrastructures—such as **regional health information organizations (RHIOs)** and the **national health information network (NHIN)**—that work together to achieve fully interconnected electronic healthcare records, in which previous test results, medications, and treatments are recorded for future reference.

Health information management (HIM): The management of medical records in multiple formats (paper, scans, tracings, images, electronic) for ready access for patient care, reimbursement, and research.

Health Information Technology for Economic and Clinical Health (HITECH) Act: Part of **ARRA** that includes incentive payment for adoption of **meaningful use of certified EHRs.**

Health Insurance Portability and Accountability Act (HIPAA) of 1996: A federal law aimed at protecting patient privacy and facilitating patients' access to their own health records.

HIPAA-grade encryption: Encrypted data or documents according to HIPAA Security and NIST 800-66 guidelines.

HL7: A predominately volunteer organization, part of ASTM (American Standards Testing and Materials) that sets standards for Electronic Health Records, Messaging (i.e. interfaces), Clinical Document Architecture (CDA) amongst others. www.hl7.org.

Hybrid record: A combination of paper and electronic records, and other media such as film, images, and scans.

Interrogatories: Written questions in legal proceedings between opposing parties.

Late entries: Entries into the medical record for events that occur after the initial episode of care. When a late entry is documented, it should be clearly identified as a "late entry."

Legal discovery: The act or process of finding or learning something previously not known, with the purpose or intent of using it as evidence in a criminal or civil legal case.

Legal health record (legal medical record): A healthcare entity's data, documents, reports, and information that comprise the formal business record(s) that is to be used during legal proceedings and as defined for various disclosures, especially subpoenas and other court-ordered disclosure of healthcare provider business or medical records.

Legal hold: A formal legal hold is an order or other instrument from a court demanding that information (including metadata) be held inviolate and with no additions, deletions, or amendments that cannot be completely tracked and reversed. This term can also be used to describe the processes used by a healthcare provider to respond to a court ordered legal hold or as a routine step in a litigation response procedure.

Litigation response: Term used to describe the processes that are invoked if the potential for lawsuits or litigation is detected, typically triggered by atypical record disclosure requests.

Meaningful use of certified EHRs: Under ARRA, the term meaningful use refers to use of an EHR according to published criteria. Certified EHR means certification by an accreditation body, of which CCHIT (Certification Commission for Health Information Technology; www.CCHIT.org) was the first. The phrase "Meaningful use of Certified EHR" is used in reference to the criteria set out in ARRA by which a hospital or eligible professional (EP) can receive incentive funding from Medicare or Medicaid for appropriate use of a well-functioned electronic health record system.

Medical administration records (MARs): The records used to document the date and time each dose and type of medication is administered to a patient.

Medical record: A paper- or computer-based tool for collecting and storing information about the healthcare services provided to a patient in a single healthcare facility; also called a patient record, medical record, resident record, or client record, depending on the healthcare setting.

Metadata: Descriptive data that characterize other data to create a clearer understanding of their meaning and to achieve greater reliability and quality of information. Metadata consist of both indexing terms and attributes. Data about data: for example, creation date, date sent, date received, last access date, last modification data.

National health information network (NHIN): Interoperable information infrastructure that links various healthcare information systems together, allowing patients, physicians, healthcare institutions, and other entities nationwide to share clinical information privately and securely; a network of networks.

Non-repudiation: Using technology and/or business processes to create an environment where a document, data, authorship, signature, or similar action cannot be easily questioned or repudiated, especially in court. Authentication (many types) is one means of non-repudiation; encrypted digital signatures are another.

Not reasonably accessible business records: Records that are not easily accessed and that would incur considerable cost and time to retrieve.

Original document: An authentic version (as opposed to a copy).

Personal health record (PHR): Medical record kept by individuals.

Preservation order: A formal court order or other instruction to preserve data or documents in the course of litigation. *See also* **Legal Hold**.

Protected health information (PHI): A HIPAA concept of medical or billing information from a covered entity or business associate that contains one of the 18 delineated identifiers.

Public key infrastructure (PKI): A system of digital certificates and other registration authorities that verify and authenticate the validity of each party involved in a secure transaction.

Reasonably accessible business records: Records that are routinely and relatively easily accessed and that would not incur considerable cost and time to retrieve.

Record custodian: Individual who attests to the integrity of business records and supervises the release of copies or duplicates of original records for review to external parties. In practice, the record custodian also has other duties to protect and define business records, i.e. creating defined legal record sets for disclosure and assisting in evaluating EHRs for legal record functionalities.

Regional health information organization (RHIO): An organization that manages the local deployment of systems promoting and facilitating the exchange of healthcare data within a **national health information network (NHIN)**.

Release of information (ROI): The process by which a healthcare provider discloses medical record (or EHR) information to patients and third parties, with proper authorization.

Safe harbor: A legal concept where adherence to statute, rule, or regulation can result in protection from prosecution or penalty in certain well-defined situations. For example, there is a safe harbor established for proper disclosure of HIPAA Security-based encrypted PHI (Protected Health Information).

Source system: The system in which data were originally created and stored.

Spoliation: Malicious alteration, concealment, or destruction of evidence such as business records.

Subpoena: Legal request for patient information.

Subpoena duces tecum: Type of subpoena that requires the witness to bring documents to court when he or she testifies.

National Conference of Commissioners on Uniform State Laws: Group of officials that creates states laws and regulations, frequently derived from the **Federal Rules of Civil Procedure (FRCP).**

Uniform rules: Rules issued by the Uniform Commissioners that are often used as templates for state law or rules (that is, civil procedure). The FRCP and Uniform rules related to electronic records are very similar. There is also an important Uniform Rule adopted by many states—called the Uniform Photographic Copies of Business and Public Records as Evidence Act—that guides the admission of record copies into evidence and is crucial for record managers and custodians.

Workflow (Business Process Management): A class of applications that creates work lists, workgroups, and electronically manages the movement of work items and tasks using rules, triggers, and maps through work processes; often included within electronic document management systems; sometimes referred to as BPM workflow.

Appendix B

References and Resources

References

45 CFR Part 170 Health Information Technology: Initial Set of Standards, Implementation Specifications, and Certification Criteria for Electronic Health Record Technology; Interim Final Rule.

AHIMA e-HIM Work Group: Guidelines for EHR Documentation Practice. 2007. Guidelines for EHR documentation to prevent fraud. *Journal of AHIMA* 78(1): 65–68.

AHIMA e-HIM Work Group on Core Data Sets for the Physician Practice Electronic Health Record. 2003. Task force report. Chicago: AHIMA.

AHIMA Work Group on Core Data Sets as Standards for the EHR. 2004. Practice brief: E-HIM strategic initiative: Core data sets. *Journal of AHIMA* 75(8):68A–D.

AHIMA e-HIM Work Group on e-Discovery. 2006. The new electronic discovery civil rule. *Journal of AHIMA* 77(8):68A–H.

AHIMA e-HIM Work Group on Maintaining the Legal EHR. 2005. Practice brief: Maintaining a legally sound health record—Paper and electronic. *Journal of AHIMA* 76(10):64A–L.

Beaudoin, J. 2009. 'Meaningful use' no mystery, experts contend. *Healthcare IT News*. http://www.healthcareitnews.com/news/meaningful-use-no-mystery-experts-contend.

California Hospital Association. 2007. State of California Consent Manual.

Dougherty, M. 2005. Practice brief: Understanding the EHR system functional model standard. *Journal of AHIMA* 76(2):64A–D.

Dunn, R. 2007. Calculating the costs of e-Discovery. *Journal of AHIMA* 78(10):64–65,72.

False Claims Act (31 USC § 3733).

Federal Rules of Civil Procedure (FRCP): Rule 17, Appendix A, chapter 2 (2006).

Federal Rules of Civil Procedure (FRCP): Revisions and additions to Rules 16, 26, 33, 34, 37, and 45, as well as Form 35; effective Dec. 1, 2006.

Federal Rules of Evidence (FRE): Article VIII, Rule 803(6), Rule 901 (a).

Health Insurance Portability and Accountability Act of 1996 (HIPAA). http://www.hipaa.org/.

HL7 Record Management and Evidentiary Standards. 2007. http://www.hl7.org.

McLendon, K. 2010. Copy that? Meeting the Meaningful Use objectives for electronic copies, parts 1 and 2. *Journal of AHIMA* 81(4):42–43.

McLendon, K. 2007. Record disclosure and the EHR: Defining and managing the subset of data disclosed upon request. *Journal of AHIMA* 78(2):58–59.

National Conference of Commissioners on Uniform State Laws. 2007. Uniform Rules Relating to Discovery of Electronically Stored Information.

Office of the Inspector General (OIG): 5 USC App. 3 § [6][a][4].

Reich, K.B. 2007. Developing a litigation response plan. *Journal of AHIMA* 78(9):76–78,86.

Roach, W.H., R.G. Hoban, and B.M. Broccolo. 2006. *Medical Records and the Law*. Sudbury, MA: Jones & Bartlett.

Sarbanes-Oxley Act of 2002. www.soxlaw.com/.

Uniform Rules of Evidence Act (2005).

Uniform Photographic Copies of Business and Public Records as Evidence Act.

Uniform Rules Relating to Discovery of Electronically Stored information August 2007.

U.S. Code, Administrative subpoenas (18 USC § 3486).

Resources

AHIMA. 2008. Copy functionality toolkit. Chicago: AHIMA.

AHIMA e-HIM Workgroup on Best Practices for Electronic Signature and Attestation. 2009.

AHIMA e-HIM Work Group on the Legal Health Record. 2005. Guidelines for defining the legal health record for disclosure purposes. *Journal of AHIMA* 76(8):64A–G.

AHIMA EHR Practice Council. 2007. Developing a legal health record policy. *Journal of AHIMA* 78(9):93–97.

American Recovery and Reinvestment Act (ARRA) of 2009. Public Law 111-5.

Burrington-Brown, J. 2007. Legal EHR FAQs. *Journal of AHIMA* 78(9):77,80.

Electronic signature, attestation, and authorship. Appendix A: HL7 EHR-System Records Management and Evidentiary Support (RM-ES) Functional Profile Standard Excerpt. *Journal of AHIMA* 80(11).

Klein, S.R. 2007. Legal perspective: Welcome to the digital age. *Journal of Healthcare Information Management* 21(4).

McLean, T.R. 2009. Authenticating EHR metadata. *Journal of AHIMA* 80(2):40–41,50.

McLendon, K. 2006. LHRs in the electronic record age: What we know so far. AHIMA's 78th National Convention and Exhibit Proceedings.

Index